Customer Expectation Management

The focus of Customer Expectation Management is great and much needed as smart customer interactions are the driving force for sustainable value creation.
—Freddie McMahon, CEO, Decisionality Ltd

For businesses today, operational profitability is no longer enough: business success is dependant on delivering successful customer outcomes that increase loyalty, and reduce turnover and the associated high costs of customer acquisition. Customer Expectation Management shows how customer expectations exist in every point of contact, driving the necessity for repeatable business processes that align a business with its customers' success. A process-centric organization with that alignment as their goal can go beyond the mere efficiency gains of process improvement to proactively avoid failures – that is, any missed customer expectations – before they occur, and generate a high degree of customer loyalty.
—Sandy Kemsley, Principal, Kemsley Design and Author, Column2.com

Increasing globalization, trends towards decentralization and the emergence of new Internet technologies are forcing all public, private and social sector organizations into an "Experience Economy" in which your activities must be integrated with those of your customers via "Human Interaction Management." If you are an executive seeking to help your organization win in such a new and challenging environment, this book will help you develop the culture change necessary to get started.
—Keith Harrison-Broninski, CTO, Role Modelers Ltd. and Author, *Human Interactions: The Heart And Soul Of Business Process Management*

Also from Meghan-Kiffer Press

EXTREME COMPETITION:
INNOVATION AND THE GREAT 21ST CENTURY
BUSINESS REFORMATION

MORE FOR LESS:
THE POWER OF PROCESS MANAGEMENT

BUSINESS PROCESS MANAGEMENT:
THE THIRD WAVE

THE POWER OF PROCESS:
UNLEASHING THE SOURCE OF COMPETITIVE ADVANTAGE

IT DOESN'T MATTER:
BUSINESS PROCESSES DO

THE REAL-TIME ENTERPRISE:
COMPETING ON TIME

THE DEATH OF 'E' AND
THE BIRTH OF THE REAL NEW ECONOMY

Acclaim for our books:

Featured book recommendation
Harvard Business School's *Working Knowledge*

Book of the Year, *Internet World*

Customer Expectation Management

Success without Exception

Terry Schurter
Steve Towers

Meghan-Kiffer Press
Innovation at the Intersection of Business and Technology
Tampa, Florida, USA
www.mkpress.com

Publisher's Cataloging-in-Publication Data

Schurter, Terry
Customer Expectation Management: Success Without Exception / Terry Schurter and
Steve Towers, - 1st ed.
p. cm.
   Includes index.
   ISBN10: 0-929652-07-X   ISBN13: 978-0-929652-07-8
   1. Management 2. Technological innovation. 3. Diffusion of innovations.
   4. Globalization—Economic aspects. 5. Information technology. 6. Information Society. 7. Organizational change. I. Schurter, Terry. II. Title

HM48.S75 2006   2006934042
303.48'33–dc22   CIP

Published by Meghan-Kiffer Press
310 East Fern Street — Suite G
Tampa, FL 33604 USA

Meghan-Kiffer books are available at special quantity discounts for corporate
education and training use. For more information write Special Sales, Meghan-Kiffer
Press, Suite G, 310 East Fern Street, Tampa, Florida 33604 or call (813) 251-5531

Meghan-Kiffer Press
USA

Printed in the United States of America. SAN 249-7980
MK Printing 10 9 8 7 6 5 4 3 2 1

This book is dedicated to the new breed of business leaders that will build business success on customer success

The coming of a new century has introduced the convergence point for a new form of competition, one characterized by a new value chain—the 21st century value chain. In this wholly new paradigm, business will build success on customer success, rather than margin, marketing, hype, or the many other forms of market and business manipulation common in the old-school way of business management. Times change, and the change underway now will result in a new breed of business—the hyper-competitive business—that will be a boon to the global economy, while also transforming our lives into a simpler and more fulfilling consumer experience. The delivery of success without exception will do far more than just drive business success across the globe; it will enhance the quality of all of our lives.

To achieve sustainable growth and profitability requires new thinking and new actions. Businesses must empower employees at all levels of the organization to act in direct alignment with strategy, where that strategy enables the meeting of customer expectations—without exception. There are a few companies that have done this, but the cost has been high and the challenge daunting. Now there is clear guidance on how to deliver success without exception in any organization of any size and in any market. Some will choose to adopt new techniques and achieve new levels of success in their business; others won't.

This book is for those who choose to succeed.

Preface

The 21st century economy is beginning to take shape as an economy with truly global competition, customers that will settle for nothing less than simplicity and success, and a value chain that is *not* driven by margin alone.

Business success will be won by those who take innovative action to create customer success as a natural by-product of the activities of everyone in the organization. Strategy can no longer be implied in functional directives of the business; it must be explicit in the actions the people in the organization take to meet customer expectations on a daily basis.

To achieve business success requires successful execution on two new elements (along with one old one) of the new value chain, which I explain in the book. It may sound difficult, but it is not. Customers are at the heart of business success in the 21st century. This book explains where, why and how. The concepts are straightforward and actionable. Becoming a hyper-competitive business does not require a cast of superstars performing feats of strength one after another. Any business can become hyper-competitive and those that do will create success for their customers, owners and employees. It is time to put the dynamics of the 21st value chain to work for you.

Best Wishes,

Terry Schurter
Dallas. Texas, USA

Contents

LEAVE NO CUSTOMER BEHIND 9
   One Common Denominator – the Customer 10
   Make My Life Simple 11
   The 10 Commandments of the Customer-Focused Enterprise: 12
THE 21ST CENTURY VALUE CHAIN 13
   21st Century Business is NOT a Margin Game 19
   Successful Customers Lead to Successful Businesses 20
   Where Has All The Trust Gone? 23
VALUE CHAIN IMPACTS 29
   Impact on Market Potential 32
   Impact on Market Realization 33
   Impact on Margin 34
THE VALUE PROPOSITION 41
   Hotmail, Vonage and Skype 48
NEW REVENUE 51
   21st Century Value Chain Realities: 56
   New Revenue Stream – More New Customers. 57
   New Revenue Stream – Decreasing Loss Relationships 59
   New Revenue Stream – Customer Lifecycle Extension. 62
MANAGEMENT BY EXPECTATION 65
   Federal Express (FedEx) 69
   Virgin Mobile 72
TRUTH, MISSION STATEMENTS AND MANDATES 76
   The 10 Essential Truths of Customer-focused Companies: 77
   The Customer Success Mandate: 78
THE HYPER-COMPETITIVE BUSINESS 79
   Meeting Customer Expectations Without Exception: 80
   Cellular Service – Virgin Mobile USA 83
   The Budget Airline Example 84
   Success without Exception Framework: 90

Budget Airlines – A Hyper-Competitive Business *91*
The Margin Game—Learning from the Airline Industry *96*
The New Budget Airline *97*
HYPER-COMPETITIVE PROCESSES 99
The Customer Interaction Model *102*
Threat Detection and Failure Avoidance *107*
HYPER-COMPETITIVE PROCESSES AND PARTNERS 114
Best Buy *116*
HYPER-COMPETITIVE METRICS 117
THE DANGER OF UNREPEATABLE POSITIVE OUTCOMES. 122
PROSUMER PROCESSES – THE NEW FRONTIER 127
Amazon.com *130*
BECOMING A HYPER-COMPETITIVE BUSINESS.................... 131
Many Ways to Achieve Success *135*
A Controlled Approach: *136*
Get Started *137*
REFERENCES 138
INDEX 139
ABOUT THE AUTHOR 142

Leave No Customer Behind

Today, you unintentionally motivated 10% of your customers to reconsider their relationship with you (in favor of your competitors). Or was it 20%? Or 30%?

Today, you worked hard to squeeze at least some margin out of an already squeezed value chain. But how much more is there to squeeze?

Today, two foreign competitors (and one virtual) joined your already *crowded* market, stealing away part of your precious customer pool. Can you afford the loss (and cost)?

Today, you did what you could to help your business succeed, but will it?

Today, you missed the most important opportunity to leverage the one remaining strength of your business—because you didn't know what it was. Will you miss it tomorrow?

Today, you are reading this book, and that will give you the knowledge required to change tomorrow, to leverage the power hidden inside your business, to become a business that is a competitive force strictly by the nature of how you work. Today, you will learn how to Leave No Customer Behind, unleashing new low-cost revenue-streams into your business, while maximizing the real revenue of your customers. Today, you will learn how to drive actionable strategy down into every corner of your organization—no matter how large or geographically diverse it may be. Today, you will learn:

- How to unlock the hidden power in your business that can transform your company into a hyper-competitive machine
- How to produce new revenue-streams into your business

without creating any new products or services
- How to maximize the real revenue potential of your customers as a by-product that just "happens"
- How to drive actionable strategy down into every corner of
  your organization—without training, education or any other
  significant effort, and
- How to make your business successful—even in the face of
  the global competition "boom" looming on the horizon

Every business wants to succeed. People in business work
hard and they often work smart. Businesses offer more for less,
same day or next day, how you want it, where you want it, and
with more options than ever before.

One Common Denominator – the Customer

All of it comes down to one common denominator: the customer. Businesses cannot succeed without customers. Which is
why customers are king, the customer is job one, the customer
comes first, the customer is always right. Right?

No, wrong. Making the customer king, job one, first, and
always right will not make the business succeed. Even those
companies that do offer exceptional customer service are bark-
ing up the wrong tree. Too much emphasis on customer service and margin goes flying out the window, because customer
service costs money. For businesses to be successful, they
don't need to deliver exceptional customer service. They don't
need to offer exceptional value. They don't need to create exceptional products. They don't need to be exceptional at all.

But they do need to *run their business by defining and managing
customer expectations* and *delivering on those customer expectations without exception.*

Defining your business in terms of customer expectations, and then meeting those expectations without exception are the new keys to unlocking business success. Make customers successful on every interaction with the business and your customer will stay your customer. Now, that will make your business successful.

Businesses are in the business of providing products or services to their customers, or a combination of both. Defining competitive goods and services offerings with respect to customer expectations creates the opportunity for business success. And delivering on customer expectations in every interaction with the customer will produce business success—not some of the time, not most of the time, but all of the time. If you want your customers to remain your customers, give them *every reason* to do business with you and *no reason* to reconsider doing business with you. Fail to define and operate your business on competitive customer expectations—or to meet a customer expectation just once, instead of repeatedly—and that customer has been motivated to seek out your competitors. Failure to deliver on customer expectations is an invitation for your competitors to take away your customer.

Make My Life Simple

The truth is that customers want their lives to be simpler. When they engage with a business they have a goal and they have expectations. They have a mental perception of what is going to happen, what they will need to do, how long it will take and exactly what the scope of the interaction should be. Unfortunately, most businesses can't repeatedly deliver on this expectation—even when it is a simple matter to do so—

because they do not manage their business by customer expectations. They fail to define their goods and services by customer expectation, which leaves the customer with a choice of the *lesser of two evils*—making the customer choose a product that does not meet their expectation. The stark reality is that most businesses fail to put the power of the 10 Commandments of the customer-focused enterprise to work for them—the commandments that are the driving force behind business success in the 21st century.

The 10 Commandments of the Customer-Focused Enterprise:
1. Know your *target* customers—and place them first!
2. Manage your customers' expectations—regardless of who initially created those expectations
3. Define your goods and services in terms of your customers' expectations
4. Identify customer expectation metrics and criteria
5. Be laser focused on meeting your customer expectations—without exception
6. Empower your organization to deliver customer success—without exception!
7. Act before customer failure
8. Acknowledge when customer failure occurs—then tell your customer!
9. Eliminate the creation of unplanned customer expectations
10. Continuously improve on your success by continuously learning from your customers, and your employees!

To begin obeying these commandments in your business, ask yourself these questions: How many times today has your business encouraged your customers to seek out your competitors? How many times today have you motivated them to abandon their relationship with you? How many times today have you referred your customers to your competitors?

Recognize that to build sustainable success, what you're doing now is not enough. It's necessary, but it will not create sustainable business success, for if changes from global competition have not yet struck you, they will—just as they will affect your customers and suppliers. If they have struck you, well, it's going to get nothing but worse. We are only just now entering the real-time global economy. What we experience now is the tip of the iceberg. If we can't generate consistent business success from what we are doing today, then we will certainly not produce success from it tomorrow.

Will your business succeed or fail? Will you act on the knowledge you gain today? Will you define and redefine your customers' expectations as a competitive market advantage? Will you create the ability in your organization for repeatedly meeting those customer expectations?

Will you take the responsibility to make your business a hyper-competitive machine that *Leaves No Customer Behind?*

The 21st Century Value Chain

Being in business today is much different than it was in the past. Times change and many environmental factors combine to shape the requirements of business success. While the law of supply and demand remains a constant, the characteristics of supply and demand are constantly changing.

Significant events often shape the requirements for business success. For example, the Industrial Revolution and World Wars I and II dramatically altered the characteristics of supply and demand. Most of the changes affecting business success today are far more subtle, but they are no less important. The requirements for business success are changing fast enough for many organizations to already feel the impact, but slow enough that many have not recognized what is changing and how it will affect them. It is a progression representing a dire threat to business success on one hand, while offering insight and opportunity on the other.

A simple but guiding principle for twentieth-century business management was late management guru Peter Drucker's *Management by Objectives*. This powerful principle served businesses well for the fifty years since he described it in 1954, for it fit the economic and marketplace realities of the time.

In the twenty-first century, however, the realities of total global competition change the landscape of business and it's now time for *Management by Expectation*. Customer Expectation Management (CEM), which we'll explain in greater depth in this book, must now become *the* organizing principle at the very core of the business. <u>Customer Expectation Management is a business approach that identifies and shapes customer expectations, and once set by the company, those expectations must be met without exception</u>. CEM is the key to competitive advantage in the twenty-first century.

A quick review of economic principles helps to put things into perspective. Supply and demand is the foundation of the economy. Economic demand is capped by buying power, with product or service demand variation driven by perceived value and price (consumer behavior).

On the buying side of the economic model, consumers are subject to the limitations of their personal buying power. They seek to spend their money in the way that best fulfills their needs and wants from their personal perspectives. Their buying power caps their demand and their "needs and wants" drive product and service demand variation.

On the selling side, businesses constantly seek to acquire new customers through advertising and marketing, while they continually lose customers through attrition. Some attrition always exists from changes in individual needs, and even the best of customers can only be customers for life.

Business profit comes from sales price minus production costs, and is commonly referred to as margin. Businesses have costs in producing their goods and services—and they have operating expenses. They charge a price that is greater than their cost in order to produce a profit (margin).

Some businesses use creativity and innovation to create new products and new customer value propositions. This can shift portions of demand away from other products, even when the products are not related. Consumer buying power is finite, so when a new product moves into the consumer buying plan, something else is likely to move out.

These fundamental economic principles shape the nature of how businesses produce profitability. However, environmental effects can play havoc with successful business models based on these basic market elements. While economic principles remain constant, market changes can turn the requirements for business success upside-down and inside-out—completely outside the control of the businesses themselves. The power and effect of market change is much like the "force" in Star Wars: it is everywhere, it is more powerful than anything else is, we can learn to use it to our advantage, and it has a dark side.

How big are environmental impacts? Just a few decades ago, one of the most important aspects of doing business was customer service. Before self-service gas stations, discount chains, and Internet stores, businesses had to deliver customer service or patrons would not return. Customer relationships were extremely important because most businesses could reach only a limited number of customers. Geographical reach was the primary influencer of accessible market.

During this time, price was far less of a competitive factor for many businesses. Competition was limited to stores within a much smaller geographical footprint. The mail order catalog was the only means to expand territory other than building new stores. Product variation of goods by brand engendered more feature-based comparative shopping, as opposed to price. The volume of goods sold was a fraction of what it is now. Stores were smaller. Competing brands were not sold in the same store. Businesses were smaller. Each sale was important. The customer was king. Success was found in service, and businesses that served their customers well flourished.

By the 1980's, much had changed. Discount chains and department stores were expanding footprints dramatically, sales volumes were increasing, comparison shopping was reorienting on price, brands were found side-by-side in the bigger stores, product variation was dropping and customer service was a non-value added cost. Price was becoming king and volume a requirement of doing business. The small customer service oriented businesses were dropping like flies.

It was in this era that Harvard Professor Michael Porter's famous value chain analysis came into being.

In Porter's value chain analysis, value creation is based on two concepts—what the business adds to its inputs before these inputs become an output (value add) and the efficiency of the organization that determines the cost of operations. With Porter's value chain, margin is the variable that determines profitability and *margin* is controlled by performance, so performance becomes the strategic business goal.

Firm Infrastructure				
Human Resource Management				
Technology Development				
Procurement				
Inbound Logistics	Operations	Outbound Logistics	Marketing & Sales	After-sale Service

MARGIN

Porter's Value Chain

Under the volume and price market dynamics that began in the 1980's, Porter's value chain provided clear insight into how businesses could achieve profitability. In the new volume-based markets, margin was the most important factor affecting profitability. That volume and price cycle has continued unabated. More volume at a lower price has pushed margin higher and higher up the ladder of corporate importance. For example, since the 1990's, profit margins for many small commodity items such as household appliances like toasters and coffee makers, are based on cents per unit. For products like these, margin gains of only a fraction of a cent can be the difference between profitability and loss.

Margin pressures are why some very large corporations have struggled or even failed. Their inability to equal efficiency and performance levels (margin) of their competitors placed them at a competitive disadvantage. With the fading of geographical boundaries, businesses are now forced to compete with the leanest and meanest margin competitors in whatever part of the world they may be found. This is the first part of the hard reality of doing business in the 21st century.

Price competition automatically creates shrinking margins and forces price ubiquity. Competing on price alone is the least defensible business position in a global marketplace, and we are certainly experiencing a rapid acceleration in marketplace globalization. This places new stresses on businesses that experienced growing profitability from performance improvements in the 1980's and 1990's that are now seeing profit margins shrivel from competitive pricing pressures. And it's going to get nothing but worse. Efforts at performance improvements often now struggle unsuccessfully just to retain old margins in the face of falling prices. Just look at the prices for general consumer goods. Many cost less now than they did ten years ago. In this business environment, the only balancing factor is to increase sales volume. Volume multiplied by margin determines if the business succeeds or fails.

In the 21st century, margin is no longer a factor strong enough to determine success. Continued contraction of cost variance and price range are funneling companies into a zero-sum game they cannot afford to play. Businesses can no longer compete successfully on margin alone. The value chain of the business has changed, and that change reflects new requirements regarding the relationship with the customer.

Cost Variance /Price Range Contraction

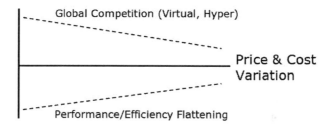

Global Competition (Virtual, Hyper)

Price & Cost Variation

Performance/Efficiency Flattening

21st Century Business is NOT a Margin Game

Is this a return to the customer service paradigm of the 1950's, 1960's and 1970's? Hardly. Customer service of those days was the delivery of additional services at the market price of the saleable good. This increases the cost of the business without an offsetting price increase. All it takes is one look at cost and price contraction to see that this will do nothing but escalate the narrowing of the funnel already closing in around businesses.

What is the answer? The answer is in the delivery of successful customer outcomes,[1] through Customer Expectation Management (CEM):

1. managing customer expectations (defining and setting expectations)
2. meeting defined customer expectations, without exception

These two activities, in combination with margin, yield a value chain that can sustain profitability in the face of our real-time, global economy brimming over with price and cost contraction—plus rapidly escalating, truly global competition. The 21st century value chain is summarized graphically in the following model.

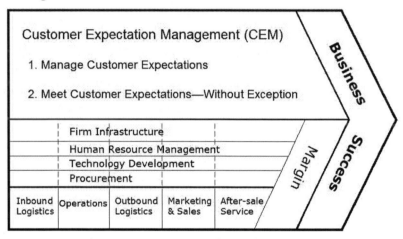

The 21st Century Value Chain

The 21st century value chain captures the fact that business success is now achieved through a combination of running the business by 1) managing customer expectations, 2) meeting defined customer expectations without exception and 3) margin (as characterized by Porter's value chain analysis).

Successful Customers Lead to Successful Businesses

Let's look at this in greater detail. What is really being represented here is that the business (any business) should be in the *business* of Customer Expectation Management (CEM). Customer expectations can also be termed customer outcomes, and certainly it makes sense to recognize that if we are in the business of delivering customer outcomes, then to be successful we must deliver *successful* customer outcomes. Successful customer outcomes meet customer expectations—that is what makes them successful—and successful customers are what make successful business.

This also means the business is no longer a goods or services business, though these are obviously an integral part of overall operations. Instead, we are in the business of defining and shaping our customers' expectations, then meeting their expectations. We use our goods and services simply as the means of meeting those expectations.

That explains the general concept of Customer Expectation Management. But if we are in the business of managing customer expectations, then we better be very good at meeting those expectations. That is the second part of CEM in the new value chain model, *meeting customer expectations without exception.* It is one thing to identify customer expectations and to manage the business based on those expectations; but if we don't meet those expectations we have failed to create any value for the customer, and the business. Not only must we meet customer expectations, we must do so without exception. Every time an exception occurs it means we have failed to deliver to our customer what we promised.

Margin, on the other hand, enables competitive positioning of goods and services *by price* if and only if a company can secure a profitable margin at market prices. Where margin used to be the first place to go when seeking profit increases and competitive pricing advantages, it has now become an enabler (rather than a driver) of success for business. Margin ensures that the business can create competitively priced products with a profit margin, but it does not provide the means to get and retain customers.

So what has changed? Why the sudden emphasis on customers and customer expectations?

In *Extreme Competition,*[2] Peter Fingar claims that customers are not only king, they have become dictators. Given unlimited choice and convenience, customers have learned new behaviors in their consumption of goods and services. Brand and business loyalty have eroded to an almost inconsequential level of impact on customer motivation and buying influence. Expectations are continuously on the rise and dissatisfaction has never been higher. These new customer dictators expect far more than most businesses can give and have translated this expectation to a devastating new one—the expectation that the business *will fail them*, and that they will need to try someone else. We are in a climate of adversarial customer-to-business relationship—and the customer holds all the cards.

Do you have family members over 70 years old? If so, ask them to recall where they shopped for appliances, tools, clothes, and other goods when they were younger; when they had young children still in school. Ask them where the best places to shop used to be back then. What stores they trusted. Ask about brands, what brands they had confidence in, which ones they would buy, and which they would not. Maybe the most striking thing is that they will be able to answer such questions with some precision.

A typical response of the times would have been: we shop at Sears; we are loyal to Sears; we go to Montgomery Wards if

Sears doesn't have what we want; we only buy Chevrolet cars; we trust Maytag; and so on.

Now ask yourself the same set of questions.

The common response now is: I shop in at least three competing stores before I buy; the service is bad; I don't trust any of them; products are not what they are advertised to be; you can get a lemon from anybody; and even if I find something I want in a store I can probably get the same thing online cheaper.

Where Has All The Trust Gone?

The point is that 50 years ago there was strong trust and affinity between customers and businesses. The customer life cycle was very long and a business had to fail the customer many times before that chain of loyalty would ever be broken. Now every link of the loyalty chain has been shattered. There is no loyalty chain and there is no forgiveness. Businesses are now at the mercy of their customers—and their customers have no mercy.

Businesses have lost control—even simple predictability—over the customer relationship. That condition, more than any other, is the most serious threat to the success and future viability of business. In some cases, the situation with the customer relationship is so dire that only the most extreme business tactics can squeeze enough out of the customer relationship to produce some degree of profitability and growth.

An example of this is the cellular telephone industry. Cellular service providers in the US are jammed between the proverbial "rock and a hard place." At the heart of the dilemma is the customer expectation.

The expectation is service related—the actual cellular service being provided by companies such as Verizon, Cingular and Sprint PCS. The specific characteristics of the unmet customer expectation include service availability, dropped calls, and service quality.

No cellular provider in the US is able to meet the customer expectation without exception, and for good reason.

They cannot meet the expectation due to a variety of factors both within their control (e.g. signal towers, signal handling technology) and outside of their control (e.g. sunspots).

How many cellular service customers know what a sunspot is and that it can cause calls to be dropped? How many people know that these sunspots are a common occurrence?

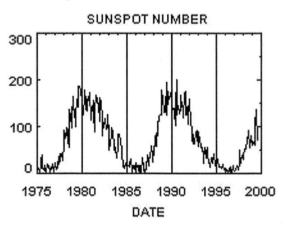

Service availability, reduction in dropped calls, and service quality continue to show ongoing improvement by every cellular provider. Yet, the customer expectation still outstrips the capability of what these companies can deliver so the gap between what the cellular service providers deliver and what their customers expect remains. This seems to be an unfair and even insurmountable barrier to business success, but before drawing that conclusion, we must ask: Where did this expectation come from? The shocking answer is that this expectation has been set by the cellular service providers!

Cellular service providers have engaged in pervasive marketing campaigns on exactly these service issues with clever messages that directly promise or commit to little or nothing, but *suggest* all and more.

The problem with this business approach is that customers don't care about the fact that "technically" nothing specific was promised or committed to by the business. Customers grasp the suggestion, and that suggestion forms their expectation. The result is that cellular service providers have created the customer expectation that the providers cannot meet without exception.

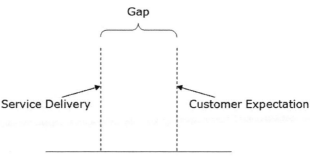

Cellular Service Expectations

The results from this disparity are dramatic. In an industry where the majority of all people qualify as likely customers and where customer motivation is strongly driven by the unique value of the service (cellular phone service offers unique benefits over other communication options), the business opportunity is tremendous—yet unrealized.

More often than not, cellular phone service providers end up in an adversarial relationship with their customers. With yearly churn rates being among the highest of any industry (ranging from 20+% to 35+%, with the churn rate being the percentage of customers that switch to a competitor), cellular service providers accept the fact that there is substantial likelihood customers will leave the relationship at the end of the service contract.

Again, this is due to the inability of the cellular service providers to meet customer expectations where the customer expectation was *set by the cellular service providers*. Early marketing moves in the industry focused on improvements or advantages in service availability, reduction of dropped calls and quality of service. These improvements are very real.

However, customers don't understand the complexity of providing cellular service—and they don't care. When cellular service providers use these improvements in service as part of their marketing pitch to gain more customers (greater market share), they inadvertently reinforce the idea that customers should expect service everywhere, no dropped calls and crystal-clear quality of service. That cycle has never stopped.

That's right, they are still "raising the bar" and giving us "the most reliable network," creating the expectation for the customer that they can deliver improved services that, in fact, they cannot deliver. It's those darned sunspots again.

What is the result? The industry suffers from excessive churn and service contracts are a mandatory requirement for most cellular providers to achieve even moderate net income.

The situation is so extreme that cellular service providers have had to take very hard business positions to achieve any profitability. When cellular phone number portability removed the *number one* factor affecting customer lifecycle duration, the industry moved to push, extend and tighten-up service contracts as a way to gain profitable customer lifecycle duration.

The business case is so upside-down that in many situations, existing customers no longer rate as a service priority to the cellular business. New customers receive priority attention because they represent one or two years of new income, while existing customers are often ignored as they are already locked in—and will likely leave at the end of their contract anyway.

Retail outlets can even be found with long lines of existing customers waiting for service, while one, two or even three new customer representatives idly stand by waiting for the next potential *new* customer to enter the store.

The thinking goes that if the customer is already likely to leave the relationship, why care? If the new customer is where profit lies, then that is where the effort must go.

These businesses know they cannot deliver on the expectations they have created. They know they cannot unleash hyper-competitiveness within their organizations because they are already upside down with the customer. Their recourse? Service contracts. Locking customers into service contracts of sufficient duration to push the customer over the loss-to-profit transition point is the business practice being employed.

The limitations of this approach are clear. Profitability remains low and is tightly restricted. There is no opportunity to add new, low-cost revenue-streams because the customer relationship is driven by contractual obligation—not success. Cellular providers are trapped in a constricted business model that leaves them vulnerable to competitive threats. Cellular providers cannot execute on the 21st century value chain because they have eliminated any chance of delivering on customer expectations without exception through setting unrealistic customer expectations with their customer acquisition strategy.

But in the new value chain, equalizing the playing field and rebalancing the relationship between the customer and the business is vital. Running the business by managing customer expectations, and meeting those expectations without exception, are the keys to opening the door to business success.

This brings up another important aspect of business in the 21st century. In the new value chain, "margin" has been replaced by "business success" as the value the business creates in the overall value chain. Margin, as presented by Porter, becomes a secondary component of delivering on business success. The new component of the value chain—Customer Expectation Management—is the force that drives the opportunity to leverage the margin portion of the chain that most businesses are already addressing.

Without adding Customer Expectation Management to the traditional focus on margin, the new value chain is unable to perform its intended function of achieving business success. Taken together, these two ingredients directly impact the profitability, customer growth, and financial growth of the business—and that is business success.

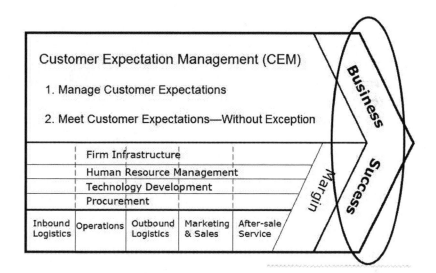

Value Chain Impacts

To achieve business success in the 21st century requires that all CEM and margin activities of the value chain be leveraged fully. Continuing to leverage only the margin-based value creation capability of the organization will rarely produce any sustainable competitive advantage, business growth, or increase in profitability. Improving margin is a valuable and essential activity of business success, but it is no longer the primary driver behind that success. Instead, it is a secondary driver, and it is the least dynamic driver with respect to competitive differentiation, business growth and profitability.

Customer Expectation Management offers the dynamic opportunities to drive business growth, customer lifecycle duration and competitive differentiation. Every organization acts on these aspects, but the problem is that most don't know it and subsequently fail to leverage the value creation potential these activities represent. Businesses incorporate elements of the value chain into their activities but the bigger picture of the value chain is not there. The result is a lot of work for a marginal result.

To understand this better it helps to place the drivers of the 21st century value chain into perspective within the context of common organizational activities. There are three layers or phases of activity in the organization defining the potential and realized value creation of the business (business success) for a given good or service. Those three phases are:

- Phase 1 (strategy) – Definition of the Value Proposition of the good or service
- Phase 2 (operational framework) – Deployment of the process that delivers the good or service
- Phase 3 (operations)– Organizational performance in delivering the good or service

These phases are shown in the following diagram, Layers of the Customer-focused Enterprise. The diagram illustrates the three phases (or layers) where activities affect the potential and realized business success of all goods or services offered by a given business.

The first phase (strategy)—creating the value proposition— is the strategic planning activity of the business. Every good or service in every business has a value proposition that defines the scope of what is to be delivered with that good or service to the customer. Anytime an organization changes an existing good or service, adds a good or service, repackages a good or service or creates a new good or service this creates a new value proposition. In simplest form, phase 1 determines *what the company will do.*

Layers of the Customer Focused Enterprise

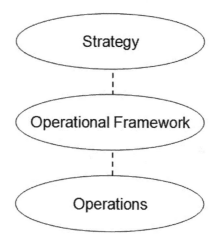

The second phase (operational framework) determines how the good or service is delivered by the business. Here is where the delivery process for the good or service of the business is determined, setting the structure within the organization that will be used to deliver the good or service as a product ready for consumption by the customer. It doesn't matter if the business thinks of this as a composite process, a number of processes or simply the way things are done. The activities a business undertakes to deliver a good or service—inclusively—is the process behind the product. This must exist for the good or service to be something the business can deliver. Phase 2 determines *how the company will do it.*

The third phase (operations) is the actual creation of the good or service including all activities and work performed by the people in the business to produce the good or service. The performance of the business in the process behind the product determines the operational margin (profit per sale). Phase 3 is *what the business actually does.*

The accumulative effect on the value chain of the business from each of these phases impacts business success on three levels:

- Market Potential
- Market Realization
- Margin

Impact on Market Potential

Creation of the value proposition is a strategic activity of the business, occurring in phase 1 of the customer-focused enterprise. The value proposition determines the maximum market for a given good or service—the market potential. Market potential is the macro set of customers and units per customer that are possible based on the value of the good or service. Market potential is not the total market; it is the potential market for a good or service based on the competitive landscape of the market—the market potential of an individual business's product offering.

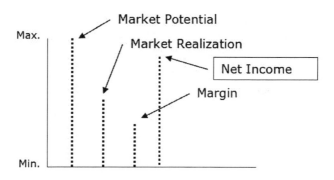

Phase Impacts on Business Success

Impact on Market Realization

Deployment of the process behind the product determines how much of the market potential can actually be realized. Where the strategic value proposition sets the value concept in phase 1 of the customer-focused enterprise, the operational framework that defines the activities, operations, methods, and structure for actually producing the good or service is defined in phase 2. Moving from strategic vision to the operational framework is a point of transition, one that must translate the strategic ideal into operational capability. Where strategy in phase 1 is based on the general capabilities of the business, the operational framework in phase 2 must incorporate people, process and systems in the creation of the framework that will deliver on the vision. This transition can be very difficult at times. In many cases the strategic vision may not cleanly translate to the operational framework or the operational framework may have numerous dependencies within it that directly impact the resulting output (the good or service) of the framework.

These effects reduce the ability of the organization to deliver on the idealistic vision of the strategic value proposition. The degree in which the operational framework can support the strategic vision, with respect to the value proposition of the good or service, determines actual market realization.

Impact on Margin

Phase 3 of the customer-focused enterprise is the actual operation—or work—that is performed in the delivery of goods and services to the customer. This is where margin is determined, with the efficiency, quality and performance of operations determining the margin per unit of the goods or services produced by the customer.

The 21st century value chain ties directly into the layers of the customer-focused enterprise and the primary drivers of the value chain. Doing business by customer expectation is a strategy activity. The setting of customer expectations that the business intends to deliver on determines the market potential.

Meeting customer expectations without exception can only be achieved if the operational framework of the organization is designed to support this goal. How the operational framework is designed in support of this goal determines the degree of market realization. The best operational framework will empower the people in the organization to meet customer expectations without exception, and that will produce the maximum possible market realization (as set by strategy).

The relationship of the 21st century value chain and the layers of the customer-oriented enterprise are presented in the following the diagram.

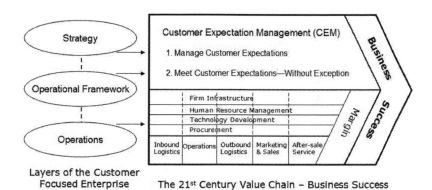

Layers of the Customer
Focused Enterprise   The 21st Century Value Chain – Business Success

Do we understand that at the heart of business success in the 21st century is the customer? We should, considering that both market potential (set by doing business based on customer expectations) and market realization (set by meeting customer expectations without exception) are clearly customer-focused activities. These activities determine both the probable and actual market-share a given product or service will achieve. Yet there is one important piece that is missing from this picture, a piece that has as much or even more effect on business success than any other. The missing piece of the picture is the fact that while the customer is at the heart of business success, at the heart of the customer is "success." Market potential and business success are capped by the degree of ability of the business in delivering "customer success"—a condition that requires that the business meet customer *expectations*.

What the 21st century value chain shows us is that the real issue at stake is the customer relationship. To achieve business success requires that businesses increase the number of customers they have and the duration of the customer-business relationship. The potential benefit to the business from increasing the number of customers a business has, and the duration of the customer-business relationship, far exceeds the potential benefit from increasing margin. Considering the continually escalating margin squeeze, increasing the number of customers and the duration of the customer lifecycle has the potential to be the primary driver of business success.

But businesses know this. They know that increasing the number of customers they have, and extending the duration of the customer lifecycle will increase revenue and can increase profitability. Many initiatives and directives are undertaken for just these reasons. Yet these initiatives and directives focus on classical business thinking in functional management structures. They are costly and difficult to manage, further requiring extreme diligence in maintaining such initiatives when they are successful. More often than not, functional management initiatives are not even focused on the right issues.

The enemy is failure – the failure to meet the "customer expectations." The challenge rests in the fact that every customer interaction can produce failure to meet expectations, and each time a failure occurs the customer relationship has been placed in jeopardy.

To be clear, the "customer" is the business's "target" customer, not the "whiner," "complainer" or other one-off characters that refuse any reasonable definition of success. There may also be customers that are reasonable but expect more than a given business has committed to deliver. These are not the business's customers.

However, for targeted customers, the challenge is to stop giving them reasons to abandon their relationship with the business. In fact, what we really want to do is to stop giving them reasons to think about the relationship in an evaluative way. What better customer relationship is there than the one where the customer simply does business with us without even thinking about other options?

Unfortunately, consistent failure to deliver on customer expectations continually encourages customers to be frustrated and critical of the businesses they buy from. Each failure to meet expectations motivates customers to abandon their relationship with the business. Failure to meet customer expectations—and subsequent motivation for customer abandonment—on a daily basis is the *current state* for most businesses. The only thing saving many businesses from critical business failure is the failure of competitors to meet customer expectations as well. Business survival rests on the fact that there is no business that delivers on customer expectations without exception. This places businesses in the competitive scenario of vying for the honor of being the "lesser of two evils."

Is being the lesser of two evils a reasonable strategic goal for your business?

Why is this? The opportunity the customer relationship offers (by delivering on customer expectations) remains largely untapped because businesses are not geared for meeting customer expectations without exception. To leverage this opportunity requires changes that currently remain outside the scope of the tools and practices being used in the attempt to improve business success.

The point is obvious even in the use of newer mechanisms based on process. Process thinking and business process management are the new wave of tools and techniques being employed by organizations in the quest for business success.

Business process management (BPM) and process thinking do address the integration of the enterprise across functional boundaries. They even extend (at times) out to the end-to-end process approach that results in a customer outcome. But in far more cases these techniques are being limited to the performance and efficiency mindset. When this happens benefits are restricted to one driver of the value chain—margin.

This leaves the business one dimensional and incapable of delivering any sustainable benefit against the goal of business success. This is the classical "leap-frog" margin game where businesses make short-term cost reductions that temporarily increase profit, competitors then catch up, prices drop, and then we go back to the margin well seeking additional cost reduction. Being caught in this cycle is a very dangerous business game to play.

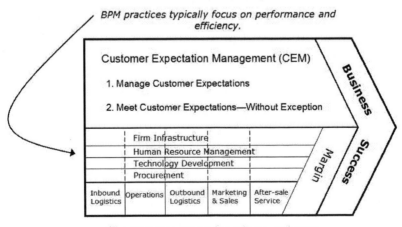

The 21st Century Value Chain and BPM

The opportunity to achieve real and sustainable business success becomes clearer when we look further into the dynamics of the 21st century value chain. Business success from the value chain occurs in four distinct areas:
1. Increasing existing customer retention
2. Increasing new customer acquisition
3. Expanding the customer relationship
4. Improvement in margin

The goal of existing customer retention is to retain 100% of all existing customers that fit the "target" customer profile of the business as a natural byproduct of the way the company works. Jumping through hoops on a case-by-case basis for each customer is not what is implied here. That approach will not yield sustainable business success.

The goal of new customer acquisition is to increase both the number of potential customers (the new customer pipeline) that transition to customers, as well as the size of the pipeline itself.

The goal of expanding the customer relationship is to increase the duration of the customer lifecycle and to increase the range (or breadth) of transactions between the customer and the business. For those companies that deliver exceptional customer success as a matter of business practice, the opportunity to expand the customer relationship is always waiting. Customers willingly "tune in" to new products or services being offered from these businesses. The positive nature of the relationship makes relationship expansion a natural affair.

The goal of margin improvement is to maximize profit from the commercial relationship with the customer and to ensure that the business can remain competitive in the pricing of its products.

The "domain of business success" is set by the new activity of CEM in the 21st century value chain. It is this activity of the value chain that determines success of customer retention, new customer acquisition and expansion of the customer relationship. When customer retention, new customer acquisition and expansion of the customer relationship all increase (and margin leverages that success to produce profit) the result is *business success.*

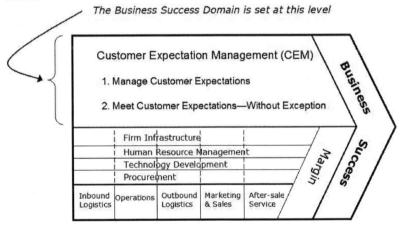

The 21st Century Value Chain – Success Domain

The new demands (and opportunity) of the 21st century value chain require that businesses meet customer expectations without exception. To do this, businesses must have a strategic vision built on customer expectations. They must also create an operational framework that translates strategic vision to operational capability without error, one that remains in explicit linkage with strategic vision. But how can organizations achieve this? It appears to be a daunting task. How can an established organization act on the 21st century value chain to produce business success without reinventing themselves? How can any organization deliver success without exception for something as complicated as customer success?

The answer lies in doing business by customer expectation (executive strategy) that explicitly informs and empowers the organization to meet customer expectations without exception. Customer success can be a naturally propagating behavior of how the business does "work." The fundamental techniques are far simpler than most people expect. Achieving this change does not require reinvention of the organization. Businesses already have the skills and capabilities to achieve this change. They simply need to apply them in the right way. That "way" will be discussed in detail later in this book but first, let's look deeper into the new elements of the value chain that have been presented here.

The Value Proposition

Every business offers something of value to its customers. This is its value proposition. The value proposition of the business determines the scope or breadth of its potential customer pool.

Goods or services offered by a business fall into one of three categories with regard to customer value. Businesses lead their market (set the customer expectation), they match the market (are on par with the customer expectation) or they lag the market (offer a value-proposition that is less than the customer expectation).

Is it clear that the value-proposition equates to the customer expectation? Creating a product that is different from competitive offerings—but that doesn't add value to the customer—won't produce success. It is the value to the customer that affects the customer buying decision. *The product value proposition and customer expectation are one and the same.*

Therefore, the company that offers the most compelling customer expectation (value proposition) has the largest potential market. Executive strategy must lead the business by driving strategy in relationship to customer expectation (value proposition). Strategically looking at the business with respect to customer expectations is the first step in preparing to leverage the 21st century value chain. Businesses either lead the market, are on par with the market or they lag the market in their value proposition to the customer.

Businesses that increase their value-proposition add new potential customers to their customer pool. They now meet customer expectations for people whose expectations they did not meet previously. Of course, they still meet lesser expectations, so they do not lose any of the existing customer pool. They also have fewer competitors. Meanwhile, those companies offering a substantially lower value-proposition are pushed further and further out of the market.

Once strategy is set by customer expectation, an increase in the expectation increases the size of the potential customer pool while decreasing the number of competitors that are able to meet that customer expectation. The value proposition (customer expectation) is the strategic element of the 21st century value chain that determines where a business sits on the customer pool/competitor graph for its market.

Businesses in the "lead" category have the largest potential customer pool, as well as the least number of competitors. Increasing the value-proposition (customer expectation) increases the size of the potential customer pool, and at the same time, it also decreases the number of competitors that can meet the customer expectation.

Value proposition leaders also benefit from the opportunity to "cherry pick" their market when desired, enabling them to build tight relationships with high value customers prone to engaging in broader relationships with the business.

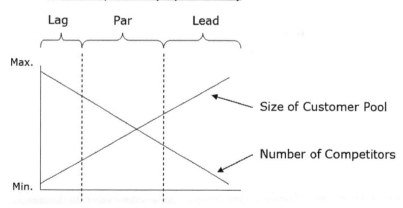

Customer Pool/ Competitor Graph

Businesses in the "par" category (the category where traditional management practice often focuses) have a large customer pool and strong competition. This is the largest market category, is where many businesses employ margin-based value-chain management, and is where BPM has been a key tool and technique in gaining margin increases.

Businesses in the "lag" category offer sub-market value-propositions and are either small niche players or are in a fight for their very survival. Practically everyone competes with them, although they are competitive with almost no one. The customer pool is small and expensive, sometimes costing the business more in customer acquisition costs than the business ever makes from new customers.

Defining the value proposition sets the scope of the product that is to be delivered to the customer, which in turn sets the size of the potential customer pool and the number of competitors for the business.

Discount Tire and Auto. Witness Discount Tire and Auto, a national retailer of tires for automobiles and light trucks. Founded in 1960 with six sets of tires (four of them recapped), this privately held company now books over $1.5 billion in revenue per year.

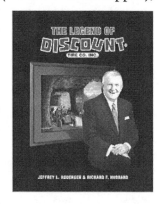

In a crowded market of big chains and long-established tire service centers, Discount Tire has risen to be the undisputed gorilla of the retail tire industry. How did Discount Tire do it? The company recognized the importance of doing business by customer expectation, and implemented executive strategy that redefined customer expectations for the tire industry. Then it delivered on those expectations without exception.

How did Discount Tire redefine the customer expectation? We can "back engineer" the Discount Tire story by considering the characteristics of the tire industry. For starters, tires are an expenditure that is a need, not a want. Tires suffer normal wear and tear that leads to the need for replacement. We know that and accept it.

However, it is often the case that the need for tires carries certain negative issues with it. We need tires, but we don't want to spend our money on tires, and we don't want to go through the time loss and hassle of getting them.

Add to this scenario that the old business model was an up-sell. Tire companies would run ads for cheap tires, then use safety, wear, ride, and so on to up-sell each customer once they were at the store—along with *other* services. This was the model of the tire industry when Discount Tire entered the market.

Somewhere along the way Discount Tire decided to change things. Looking at the market from the customer point of view, Discount Tire decided to run its business by creating a definition for success (customer success) that fulfilled an unmet need in the market. Discount Tire decided to do *customer expectation management*. This led to the creation of a new value proposition based on this unmet customer need. The customer expectation that Discount Tire decided to run its business by consisted of low prices without up-sell, the employment of staff trained to give objective advice on tire selection appropriate to the needs and goals of each customer and prompt, courteous delivery of services.

This reset the customer expectation to an entirely new level, one based on the customer point of view—and that made customers successful. The powerful insight of Discount Tire enabled it to run its business by customer expectation and its commitment to this vision enabled the company to create an organization that delivered on that customer expectation at a very high level.

How do you get to $1.5 billion in a crowded, low-margin business like retail tires? Not by adding in extra services. That is another big difference with Discount Tire. The company became an organization of tire experts. It only does tires and tire related services. You can't get your oil changed at Discount Tire because oil changes are not related to tires.

But the other side of the coin is meeting customer expectations. Discount Tire has clearly set customer expectations through its value proposition. What translates that value proposition into business success is the fact that the company delivers on the customer expectation they have created without exception (or at least at a very high level).

Another interesting move by Discount Tire was the decision to deliver flat tire repair to customers for free. Again, focusing on the customer and customer success, Discount Tire decided to give away a high-value (to the business) industry service— the repairing of customers' flat tires—for free, to all of their customers.

Discount Tire is the company that fixes its customers' flat tires for free, doesn't up-sell, offers very low prices on a broad selection of tires, has objective tire experts for employees, and gets you in and out fast.

That value proposition and delivery of success turned the tire sales and service industry upside-down.

The result is that in a crowded market with strong competitors, Discount Tire moved out to the *lead* category of the customer pool and competitor graph with its value proposition, increasing the size of its potential customer pool while reducing the number of its competitors. By delivering on expectations without exception, Discount Tire increased its conversion rate for its pipeline (new customer acquisition) and kept those customers—extending the duration of the customer lifecycle. Discount Tire customers often have a very long customer lifecycle with a significant percentage who never consider taking their business elsewhere.

So the expanded new customer stream quickly transitioned to an expanded stream of customers with a very long lifecycle. That triggered reputation and word of mouth, which pushed more new customers into the Discount Tire pipeline.

The result? A $1.5 billion a year retail tire chain gorilla emerged from just six sets of tires.

Many of Discount Tire's competitors now offer a similar value proposition to their customers. They do so because they have to—because Discount Tire made them change their offerings. Discount Tire redefined the customer expectation by choosing to do business by setting customer expectations, backed by meeting customer expectations without exception. Discount Tire did this by choice. The rest of the industry did this by necessity in order to stay in business at all.

Discount Tire remains the gorilla in the tire sales and service market even after competitors have moved to meet the customer expectations set by Discount Tire. Why is this so? Because Discount Tire chose to do business by customer expectation and it chose to deliver on expectations without exception. Competitors responded to pressure that forced them to change against their will. These companies are only responding to market pressure. They do not operate their businesses by customer expectations; they operate their businesses by competitive pressure. Their competitor (Discount Tire) sets their strategy for them.

The importance of the Customer Pool and Competitor Graph is not lost on the movers and shakers of the business world. What is clear to these people is that anytime a business can push itself far enough out on the leading edge of the graph, they position their business to have the largest market possible with the least number of competitors. Who besides Discount Tire and Auto has figured this out?

Hotmail, Vonage and Skype. Communications services represent one of the largest markets by customer count because communication is part of our everyday lives. Back in 1995, an entrepreneurial business redefined the value proposition of a relatively new communication form that was fast reaching the point of ubiquity. That form of communication was email.

The Hotmail value proposition was extremely powerful. Hotmail offered the means to access email from any computer with an internet connection because it was Web-based (as opposed to software requiring download and installation on each computer). Taking the CEM approach, they delivered ease of use (keep my life simple), convenience (any computer with an internet connection) and reduced cost (basic service is free— only buy extras you need) in the new customer value proposition. That value proposition was so strong that Hotmail signed 6.5 million subscribers in 14 months. The company changed the entire email industry, resulting in the acquisition of the company by Microsoft.

Web-based email is now a de facto requirement for email providers, while Hotmail is still growing, with over 30 million subscribers to date.

Vonage is a notable new Internet telephone provider. The value-proposition offered by Vonage is primarily a price-based resetting of the customer expectation with unlimited service over a broad geographical footprint at a price below that of local phone service from traditional phone service suppliers. Vonage also offers very low cost-per-minute rates for areas outside the included plan footprint, including international calls. To date Vonage has acquired over 1.5 million active lines. Vonage applied CEM within a limited scope, the offering of industry standard services at a greatly reduced price.

But while Vonage has made inroads into the phone market by resetting price in the traditional phone service model (and with questionable ability to make profit doing so) others have approached the customer expectation in a different way. In 2003, a PC-to-PC type of phone service was brought to the market by a company called Skype.

Skype is doing business based on customer expectations, applying CEM in a broad and unlimited way. The approach taken by Skype is simple, yet incredibly market-disruptive and powerful. Skype has taken the view that basic telephone service is more than just a commodity; it should be a free service.

What? How can a telephony provider offer basic telephone services for free? Isn't that the core service of the business?

Skype recognized that Internet technology and global connectivity enables the offering of telephone services from PC-to-PC as a free service. The basic Skype service allows anyone with a PC, speakers and microphone, or headset to talk to anyone else with a PC at no charge.

Skype delivers on the company's new customer expectation without exception through a service that reliably offers high quality voice communication, is simple to sign up for and is easy to use. The service is uniquely designed to support millions of users at very low cost to the company. In March 2006, over 6 million Skype users were on-line simultaneously.

Skype laid claim to over 100 million registered users by the end of March, 2006. The new value proposition from Skype includes the ability to talk to any Skype member anywhere for free, with very good clarity, to easily manage who can talk to you, to see if your contacts are available and a number of other capabilities such as Instant Messaging (IM), conference calling, easy muting, and even file transfers. Additional services such as personal greetings, voicemail, and the ability to call regular phone numbers (not PCs) are premium services that can be purchased when desired. Skype was purchased by eBay for $2.6 billion in the fourth quarter of 2005.

These examples demonstrate the market power of redefining customer expectations. This represents what, from the traditional Telco's point of view, is the giving away for free of something that has been their main revenue generator. In the case of Vonage, the redefining of the customer expectation is a forward movement on the already established scales of expectation from phone services providers. Vonage is competing on an improved version of an existing value proposition.

For Hotmail and Skype, the value proposition is a completely new set of customer expectations—a new value proposition that pushed them to the outer edges of the customer pool and competitor graph. By pushing outward in redefining the value proposition, Hotmail and Skype experienced the customer acquisition benefits of broad market appeal with little or no competition at the value proposition they produced. This is the dynamic behind 6.5 million subscribers in 14 months (Hotmail) and 100 million members (Skype) – as compared to 1.5 million customers in 5 years (Vonage).

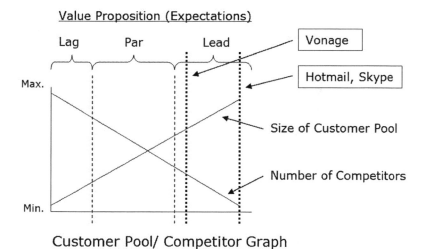

Customer Pool/ Competitor Graph

New Revenue

While activities in defining the value proposition set the market potential for goods and services, the deployment processes set the limits on how well the organization can achieve customer success—e.g. how well the business delivers the value-proposition to the customer.

Obviously, if deployment within the business is incapable of delivering on the value-proposition consistently, then there is a gap between the targeted or advertised value and the delivered value. Considering what we have already covered, this is obviously not going to go over well with customers who are dictators, have many options, offer little loyalty and are accustomed to abandoning the business-customer relationship.

The effect is a shift in where the business sits on the customer pool and competitor graph. Ineffective or inconsistent delivery of the value-proposition shifts the business to the left, decreasing the size of the customer pool while increasing the number of competitors.

Effective and consistent delivery of the value-proposition shifts the business to the right, increasing the customer pool and reducing the number of competitors. This is the first market realization impact that affects the overall success of the business.

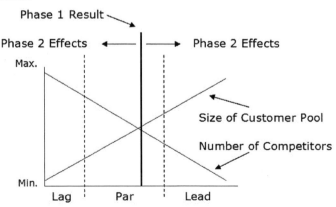

Customer Pool/ Competitor Graph
Effects from Deployment

Even when we are successful in delivering on our value proposition to our customers, we can give them reason to abandon the relationship—and can even encourage them to do so. Customer expectations are not limited to just the business's value proposition. Customer expectations exist in every business-customer *interaction* that occurs—for any reason. Failing to incorporate meeting customer expectations without exception into all customer interactions leaves this dimension of the customer-business relationship uncontrolled—and uncontrollable—producing a random and unpredictable result. This is the second market realization impact that affects the success of the business. More than any other factor, this controls the behavior of the customer lifecycle. The customer lifecycle has three characteristics that produce a profound effect on the success of the business:

- Customer acquisition is an inflow to the business's actual customer pool. These are the new customers (defined as customers where no prior relationship existed) that join in a commercial relationship with the business.
- Customer attrition is an outflow from the business's customer pool. These are existing customers that choose to abandon their commercial relationship with the business.
- Customer duration (lifecycle) is the primary factor determining the magnitude of the financial relationship between the business and the customer.

Let's look at some numbers. Every business has an average customer acquisition cost (ACAC), a customer lifecycle (duration of the customer relationship) and a profitability point where acquisition costs are offset and profit begins. Obviously, if the customer lifecycle is shorter than the profitability point for a given ACAC then the business makes no profit from the relationship—in fact, the business incurs a loss.

Looking at the diagram below it becomes clear that every new customer relationship starts with a loss (the ACAC) and only transitions to profit after the relationship yields a monetary value (based on margin) that exceeds ACAC.

ACAC, Customer Lifecycle, Profit and Loss Relationship

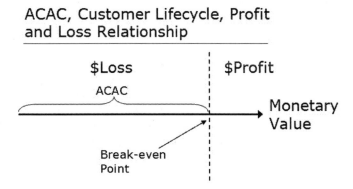

Remember also that margins are shrinking (cost variance and price contraction). This contraction in many cases requires an extension to the duration of the customer lifecycle to reach the break-even point.

Meanwhile, ACAC is also going *up*, most notably due to the number of competitors battling for each customer and the cost of advertising and marketing.

This means that every new customer starts as a loss to the business until the break-even point is crossed. Any customer that leaves the business relationship before crossing the loss-to-profit transition produces a loss for the business!

How big can these losses be? Just to get a sense for what these customer acquisition costs are consider that:

- The ACAC for e-retailers in the year 2000 was $95 with a predicted rate of $122 by 2003[3]
- For US banks ACAC is a staggering $3500[4]
- In 2001 cellular Sprint PCS reported an average ACAC of $315, [5] while competitor Nextel incurred an ACAC of $430[6]
- DirecTV reported an ACAC of $550 in 2001
- VOIP pioneer Vonage reports an ACAC of $209 (in their S1 filing they clearly show they target a 5 year average customer life to achieve profitability goals)
- In 2004 automobile franchise dealers spent an ACAC of $450 (which does not include manufacturers' ACAC or rebates)
- and the average cost per call for in-person sales calls is over $400 and that does not include the completion of a sale (new customer).

So if businesses are making double or triple digit ACAC investments in a market that has pared profit margins down to the bone, what is the value gained by keeping each customer? What is the cost incurred when the business fails to meet expectations? How can businesses achieve success when they are motivating the customer to abandon the relationship?

That being said, it not only makes a strong financial point, but it also brings us around to the old adage that tells us "it is easier to keep an existing customer than it is to acquire a new one." We don't have to compete for existing customers' attention as we do when seeking to acquire new customers. We just need to meet their expectations because we already have their attention. These are the realities of the 21st century value chain.

21st Century Value Chain Realities:

- New customers start as a loss
- New customers cost more than they used to (bigger loss)
- One failure can end the relationship, even while still a loss
- Customer success without exception is the only way to effectively stem abandonment (new and existing customers)

These realities combine to show that meeting customer expectations without exception in the new value chain impacts the business in very powerful ways:

- Increase in new customers through successful "new customer" process
- Increase in new customers—reputation, word of mouth
- Reduced attrition during loss to profit duration (reduction in loss relationships)
- Increase in profit per customer from increased duration of customer lifecycle

In the diagram below, we see how meeting customer expectations without exception makes its impact known on the success of the business (lines indicate averages). The solid line represents the baseline from current operations while the dotted line indicates how meeting customer expectations can affect the value chain.

All factors can vary significantly, depending on how well a

company delivers on customer expectations and how its competitors match up to its performance. The graph is representative of how satisfying customer expectations can affect the business results (success) from new customers for the business.

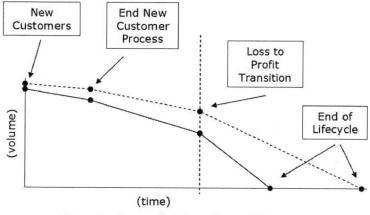

"New Customer" Value Chain Effects

The important point demonstrated here is the potential benefit that can be realized. The results can be extreme but we will look at *conservative results* to illustrate how powerful these effects really are in relationship to business success.

New Revenue Stream – More New Customers. Starting on the left, the "New Customers" point has moved slightly up the scale to indicate effects from reputation and word of mouth. This increases the total number of new customers that attempt to do business with us. This effect would typically build over time and could become very significant by itself.

Once new customers are attracted to the business, the actions required for them to complete a business transaction is called the New Customer Process. This is separated out because of its importance to the customer-business relationship. The relationship has no monetary value until this process is completed. At the "End of New Customer Process," the difference between the dashed and solid lines represents the additional number of customers the business has retained. This also represents the additional customers that have completed a monetary transaction with the business. This is new revenue.

Note that the gap at this point is much wider than at the "New Customers" point because we have delivered on customer expectations and have therefore circumvented loss of new customers. These are customers normally lost due to unmet expectations in their first transactions with the business—that have now been retained though successfully meeting expectations. There is no additional resource or capital cost expenditure to achieve this result. All that is required is the adherence to the goal of success without exception—a management practice far simpler that it may appear, as discussed in detail later.

There are no customer acquisition costs for these new customers because these are people we normally would attract from marketing and advertising, supplemented by additional customers we have drawn in by reputation and word of mouth. On the balance sheet this will show as both a reduction in ACAC (we spent the same, we just got more customers for what we spent, so the *average* cost goes down) and an increase in gross income.

Increasing the number of new customers is the first new revenue stream into the business.

So we achieve the positive result of increasing the number of new customers for the business without increasing the total cost of customer acquisition, and we achieve a higher percentage of new customers that actually complete their first commercial transaction with us (the new customer process).

In a hyper-competitive business, what matters most is how easy the business makes it for customers to deal with them. Meeting customer expectations without exception is what businesses fail to deliver, what customers desire more than anything else, and what affects the customer relationship more than all other factors combined. For example, achieving customer success without exception in the "new customer process" will increase the number of customers completing their first commercial transaction with the business, while retaining more customers for future transactions.

New Revenue Stream – Decreasing Loss Relationships. Returning to the value chain effects graph, the "loss to profit" transition point is our next milestone. The loss to profit transition point is simply the point at which profit from transactions with the customer equals the average cost of acquisition for the customer.

At this point, the gap between the dashed and solid lines has widened due to the increase in customers that have stayed in the customer-business relationship. Why wouldn't they stay? If we are meeting their expectations and if we are enabling them to be successful, then there is no reason for them to leave the relationship.

Businesses should consider new customers as investments. New customer investments start as a loss (ACAC). A percentage of new customers (losses) reach the point where revenue generated from the relationship equals the business's investment. At this point (the loss-to-profit transition) these customers are no longer a loss (though they are not yet profitable).

Businesses will always have some percentage of new customers that depart the relationship as a loss. However, reduction in that percentage indicates new real revenue that has been generated for the business.

The difference between the dashed and solid lines in the diagram below, multiplied by the average cost of customer acquisition is real new income gained. If the average cost of customer acquisition is $100 and we increase the number of new customers retained to this point by 100, the real income gained from the new practice equals $10,000.

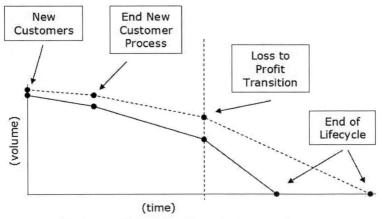

"New Customer" Value Chain Effects

Meeting customer expectations without exception increases the number of new customers entering the pipeline (the first new revenue stream). It also increases the percentage of people staying in the pipeline until they reach the loss to profit transition point, at which point we can accurately measure the revenue gain for the business.

Note the progression being presented here. The overall theme on delivering success (remember, success is meeting reasonable expectations that have been set by the strategic goals of the business) builds on itself by putting—and keeping—customers in a commercial relationship with the business. Increasing the number of customers reaching the loss to transition point increases gross revenue and gross profit (and sets up the final new revenue stream). It is a "snowball" effect, and the loss to profit transition is a point where we can measure the accumulating effect of meeting customer expectations without exception.

The increase in customers transitioning from loss to profit is the second new revenue stream into the business.

Another way of looking at the diagram is that the difference between the dotted and solid lines represents customers normally lost by failure in meeting expectations. Meeting expectations keeps these people in a commercial relationship with the business, and when they reach the loss-to-profit transition point, we can measure the full impact this has on the business.

Because these are all customers we have acquired without adding any new acquisition costs there is no additional sunk cost for this new revenue (sunk cost being money invested in customer acquisition). Because customer cost has not increased, the financial gain is the simple calculation of the difference between the dotted and solid lines times ACAC.

For example, if we normally have 100 customers per day reach this point and our ACAC is $100, if we increase the percentage of customers reaching the loss to profit transition point by 10% that would equal new gross revenue of $1000 per day—or $365,000 per year.

- 20%? $730,000
- 30%? $1,095,000
- 40%? $1,460,000

Would you like to increase your business's revenue by 10%, 20%, 30% or even more?

It is much easier to improve on the percentage of new customers that remain in the relationship with the business than it is to push more people into the new customer pipeline. New customers already in the pipeline need only have their expectations met in order to keep them in the relationship.

New Revenue Stream – Customer Lifecycle Extension. Finally, the area described by the "Loss to Profit Transition" points, the "End of Lifecycle" points and the dashed and dotted lines in the diagram below represents the additional domain of profitable commercial relationship.

Meeting customer expectations without exception will extend the average duration of the customer lifecycle. Extension of the customer lifecycle produces new revenue and new profit for the business, increasing the benefit the business realizes from the customer. The shaded area in the diagram above is the domain of additional profitable customer relationship that now produces profit on every extended transaction.

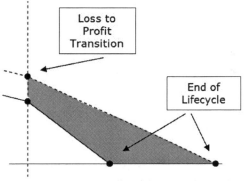

Domain of Additional Profitable Customer Relationship

Extended customer lifecycle duration is the third new revenue stream into the business.

The concept that extending the customer relationship will yield increased profitability is obvious, but what is not so obvious is the impact that occurs when we fail to meet customer expectations without exception.

Every failure to meet customer expectations, no matter what the interaction is or how it fails, creates a reason for the customer to reconsider their relationship with the business. The only "reconsideration" ever desired is for expanding the customer-business relationship into new (or more) products. Otherwise, we should never give our customers any reason to reconsider their relationship with us. Would you walk up to your fiercest competitor and ask them to please take your customers away? Unfortunately businesses do this every single day by failing to meet customer expectations.

Consider a case where the average duration of the customer relationship increases by 10%. That 10% increase in duration of the customer lifecycle increases the duration of the revenue opportunity window for the business by 10% in the *most profitable phase of the relationship*. Once we pass the loss to profit transition point the relationship becomes one of increased, profitable revenue.

How big of a deal is this? This is the proverbial *pot of gold* at the end of the business rainbow.

There is a natural lifecycle to all customer relationships, which at its longest equals the lifespan of the customer. How often these days do customers stay in any relationship with a business to the relationship's natural duration? Practically never. Failure to meet expectations drives customers out of the relationship, requiring businesses to fight for reacquisition of the customer over and over again.

Only by crossing the "loss to profit transition" with customers can business success be attained, reaching the part of the customer relationship where the business reaps success on every customer transaction. Extending the duration of the customer lifecycle by meeting customer expectations without exception will push that lifecycle to its natural limits.

What might the result be? Well, if customers currently generate $x dollars of gross profit then $x minus ACAC is the net profit from the customer. However, any increase in $x from this point is pure profit. If $x is increased by 10%, then $x times .1 is the *new net profit* the business has realized. For a business with 1000 customers whose customers generate $100 of gross profit, an increase of 10% in transaction total from increasing the customer lifecycle yields $10,000 in net profit.

Because $x is debited by ACAC to determine original profit, *the net profit for the business is actually greater than the 10% increase in transaction total.*

Management By Expectation

The 21st century value chain provides a framework for business success, and at the top of the value chain is *Customer Expectation Management.* But what is meant by Customer Expectation Management (CEM)? This is the outward-in view of the business that is focused on the customer. It's the view from the customer perspective. At the end of day, it is only the success of the customer (in the eyes of the customer) that holds any promise for sustainable business success.

This means that businesses must cast off the shackles of hierarchical and functional management. These management approaches cannot yield sustainable customer success, yet customer success is the key to business success.

Make no mistake. Just because widespread failure of customer expectations currently gives businesses room to remain profitable in these management structures, this "lull before the storm" will not last much longer. More and more businesses are getting the hyper-competitive message and those that don't will soon find themselves unable to compete in a market that has left them behind.

Customer Expectation Management means that the strategic goals of the business must be customer-focused from the outside-in. The reason the hyper-competitive business exists is to fulfill customer expectations. Thus, the business must think, plan, build, act and deliver on those very same expectations.

Business executives that take control of their own destiny understand that the business is all about meeting customer expectations, which also means the business must define those expectations it chooses to deliver on. CEM is the key.

These customer expectations are also the value propositions of the business to the customer. The definition or redefinition of customer expectations occurs anytime a company initially defines its value proposition to the customer or when it significantly alters an existing value proposition it be delivered. This definition/redefinition occurs to serve one of three purposes:

- The value proposition is redefined to <u>meet</u> the market expectation
- The value proposition is redefined to <u>reset</u> the market expectation
- The value proposition is redefined to <u>target</u> a modified customer characteristic.

It is common for businesses to redefine customer expectations. It happens every day in small increments—and in large ones, too. For many businesses, the practice of Successful Customer Outcomes (SCOs) is currently being employed to meet a market expectation set by competitors that is above the current deliverable of the business. Pain is the great motivator and market erosion from failing to keep up with competitors is very painful to the businesses lagging the market.

But the practice of setting customer expectations often starts with simply aligning the business with the customer. Customers desire success. Most have reasonable expectations even though these expectations are rarely met. Understanding the customer, their expectations and the incorporating of that knowledge into the strategic goals of the business is the starting point on the journey to becoming a hyper-competitive business. Defining the expectation (and meeting it) sets the foundation for redefining the expectation.

Why redefine the expectation? The answer is simple. Remember the customer pool/competitor graph? Where we want to be is out on the right side of that graph where we maximize the size of our customer pool and minimize the number of competitors we have.

From a foundation of alignment with the customer's expectations, the business can address competitive value proposition threats and make moves for competitive differentiation in its market. When a business operates by customer expectation, resetting expectations will provide direct, competitive benefit.

But there are levels in resetting the customer expectation. Incremental adjustments are well within the capability of all businesses. Fundamentally resetting the value proposition is an entirely different matter. This requires a willingness to engage in "forward thinking" that can challenge market perceptions regarding the value the business delivers. This often entails the provisioning of a traditional revenue-generating aspect of the business to that of a free or very low-cost benefit of the newly defined value proposition. This is not a technology-driven activity; it is a strategic activity of the people in the business.

When the value proposition undergoes change, this change must be propagated out to the customer, and inward to the people in the organization that will be responsible for delivering on the new expectation. Clearly communicating the redefined customer expectations to customers and the business's organization is commonly overlooked, yet it is critical so that:

- Customers know what to expect from the relationship
- Employees of the business know what the business has committed to delivering to the customer.

Further, in order to maximize the customer lifecycle the expectation that the business creates (intentionally or not) must match what the business delivers. Whatever the expectation is that the company tells the customer they will deliver through marketing and advertising must *be* what the company actually delivers to the customer, otherwise the customer relationship is immediately placed in jeopardy.

It's nothing new to state that customers expect to get what we tell them—or is it? Isn't it true that many (most?) customers don't expect to receive all of what a business offers and we (customers) generally have high aspirations and low expectations? The fact of the matter is that customers believe they should be able to get what businesses tell them will be delivered, but they actually expect to be routinely disappointed. Some businesses are very good at delivering on expectations they have set—and where this is the case, these companies are often leaders in their respective markets (FedEx, Discount Tire and Auto, Wal-Mart, and Dell are notable examples). But most companies don't focus on CEM, and don't factor into strategic planning the impact and power of setting, then meeting, customer expectations. The setting of customer expectations is a powerful mechanism in the quest for business success, yet the fact remains that companies have far more power than they use in setting *realistic customer expectations*.

This point is further emphasized by observations from classical marketing techniques. Some classical marketing hype methods still desire to woo customers into the fold by inferring derived benefits from products and services that are not really provided by the product. But this type of expectation creation will not yield sustainable customer relationships. Instead, this path leads to customer dissatisfaction and distrust because, like it or not, the business has intentionally deceived the customer. Granted, in some low-end, non-durable product categories it can be necessary to "jazz up" old products to keep them "fresh" but inferring that a product delivers a result that it simply does not deliver will not create customer loyalty or extend the duration of the customer lifecycle.

Departing from this classical marketing hype mentality, companies do have the means for clearly setting customer expectations. A good example of this is FedEx.

Federal Express (FedEx). The core business of FedEx (Federal Express) is the delivery of packages. The company defined the package delivery market starting in the early 1970's through a series of innovations that started by combining air and ground package transportation.

FedEx was the first company to use package drop boxes, increasing customer convenience. It was the first company to use technology for the tracking of packages, introduced the overnight letter, provided the first PC-based automated shipping system, and it was the first package delivery company to implement package barcode labeling.

As services grew, FedEx clearly set customer expectations by offering dependable delivery services that included:

- Convenience – stores, phone, drop boxes, and computer systems all gave customers easy access to FedEx for their shipping needs.

- Quality – *Delivery without exception,* setting a new standard for on time and accurate parcel delivery that reset the customer expectation for the entire industry.

- Tracking – FedEx enabled customers to have easy, real-time access to tracking information through tracking technology, management practices, and information access.

FedEx built a brand that consistently meets customer expectations. It is also the market innovator, continuously driving customer expectations upward through the implementation of new services that make life simpler for its customers.

Because of this, FedEx holds a competitive edge. It remains in the "lead" portion of the competitor graph, while its meeting of customer expectations without exception pushes more new customers into its business. FedEx is also very good at *not* giving customers a reason to consider other delivery services, which extends the duration of the customer lifecycle. These attributes maximize its business success.

What effect does this have on competitors of FedEx? Competitors (e.g., UPS, USPS, and DHL) have no choice but to compete on either, a) niche delivery services not served by FedEx or b) cost. Lower cost service is the main opportunity for competitors of FedEx, a condition that limits the market to basic delivery services where time sensitivity is lower.

That brings up another point. FedEx does not have to beat competitor pricing, it only has to be reasonable in respect to "apples to apples" competitive offerings. Because FedEx consistently resets customer expectations then delivers on expectations without exception, FedEx does not suffer from the same pricing pressure and scrutiny with which its competitors are forced to live.

FedEx is the premium delivery service (again, redefining expectations and delivering on expectations) and customers expect to pay more for the best. By keeping the price differential for "apples to apples" services close to competitor pricing, FedEx ensures that it will maximize its customer base while increasing its profitability.

For competitors, the market opportunity is limited to niche markets and competition on the margin portion of the value chain—the one place in the value chain where operating pressures drastically increase and downward profitability pressures are extreme—because FedEx leads the delivery market in Customer Expectation Management.

Redefining the customer expectation is the activity of creating step change in the goods or services the organization creates. Whenever an organization increases the overall value proposition to the customer, they have redefined the expectation of the customer. FedEx is an example of a company that has made step change in the customer value proposition a matter of habit.

In the global real-time economy, customer expectations from business shift very quickly to align with whatever the best value proposition in the market happens to be at the time. If company A offers more channels of digital television for less than the current norm (the expectation), then the customer base for digital television quickly learns of this new offering, and immediately responds with the raised expectation that all companies offering digital television service should offer this expanded set of channels at the new price point. Communication is global and instantaneous—a virtual real-time sharing of information. We are now forced to compete with whoever offers the best value-proposition as soon as that value-proposition exists.

This behavior has a profound effect on business success. The opportunity to extend market share and expand the customer relationship very quickly is driven by the ability of businesses to redefine customer expectations.

Further, the ability to remain in competitive balance with competitors is also driven by this activity, as businesses will be faced with the requirement to redefine their own ability to achieve new customer expectations in response to competitors activities that produce step change in that expectation.

Virgin Mobile. Virgin Mobile entered the US market with a bang, by offering a newly defined cellular service value proposition—pay as you go (and more).

Certainly the number one customer expectation that Virgin identified as a competitive differentiator was the elimination of the onerous "cellular service contract." The service contract is a characteristic of the existing cellular service  market loosely disguised as a "customer benefit." This "benefit" is created by making non-contract service unattractive from a pricing standpoint. Why does the service contract exist in this form? It exists as a mechanism for cellular service providers to "push" a product of predetermined customer lifecycle duration (because the industry is unable to establish profitable customer lifecycle duration due to consistent failure on customer expectations). The practice (and product) exists as a mechanism to ensure some profit to the cellular service provider.

Virgin saw this as an opportunity to define a new customer expectation that would place it at a competitive advantage for a meaningful portion of the cellular service market. Virgin introduced a new service, *pay as you go*, that requires no service contract. You simply pay as you go.

That value proposition has expanded over time with an emphasis on unique features to augment the attractiveness to the demographic Virgin Mobile USA attracted with its *pay as you go* service. It redefined its own value proposition against its target market once that target market was identified through analysis of customers that the *pay as you* go strategy attracted.

That redefined value proposition has grown around the

base value proposition of pay as you to go to include:
- Simple airtime pricing
- No hidden fees
- No monthly bills
- No contracts to sign
- You control the phone, not vice versa
- Fun-filled VirginXtras and exclusive content from MTV

The results of the strategy are compelling:
- Launched in 2002
- By November 2003 Virgin Mobile USA touted 1 million customers
- By March 2004, growth had exploded to 1.75 million customers (just 4 months after reaching the 1 million customer mark)
- By February 2005 Virgin Mobile USA's customer base had grown to 3 million customers.

These results are driven by the market behavior represented in the Customer Pool and Competitor Graph for the subsegment of the cellular service market where the pay as you go service offering meets customer expectations.

By understanding customer expectations for this subsegment of the cellular service market, developing the value proposition that meets those expectations and meeting those expectations, Virgin Mobile USA was able to carve a healthy slice out of the cellular service market pie. Today, it's in a powerful competitive position and continues to lead the industry in its target market.

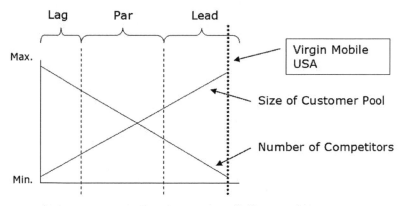

**Sub-segment Customer Pool/ Competitor
Graph for Pay as You Go Cellular Service**

Regardless of how this strategic activity is enacted within the business, for it to be actionable by the rest of the organization, the desired changes must be clear about how they affect the customer. Customer expectations for the goods or services provided by the business along with customer expectations at all customer interface points are the domain of the customer-focused enterprise. To unleash new low cost revenue into the business requires that the organization know what expectations are, how they are measured (metrics) and what constitutes success or failure.

This is can be a radical shift in how the business perceives its purpose. The customer-focused enterprise takes full advantage of the revenue streams already outlined by nature of how the business performs its work. This is a natural by-product of being a customer-focused enterprise. The goal of the organization is not just to increase the new customer pipeline, push more customers to the "loss to profit" transition, or extend the duration of the customer lifecycle. The goal is to deliver on customer expectations—large and small—without exception, with business success occurring as a natural byproduct from executing on this goal.

This is a big change in most people's "world view" of companies. The behavior and mindset of the customer-focused enterprise certainly differs from the current behavior and mindset in most businesses—a fact that stands out when we look at the Mission Statement of a customer-focused enterprise.

Truth, Mission Statements and Mandates

To help place the business approach into perspective let's look at a generic mission statement for the customer-focused enterprise. The mission statement is generic because the business tenets of a customer-focused enterprise are generic as well. It doesn't matter what business you are in, whether you produce products or services, commodity goods or specialized ones. In the customer-focused enterprise it doesn't matter *what* you do, it matters *how* you do it.

Mission Statement—We are here to deliver a customer experience that consistently produces successful customer outcomes (outcomes that meet our customers' expectations), to empower everyone in our organization with direct participation in the success or failure of delivering on that expectation, to do so at a cost level that is profitable for our business, and to periodically raise the bar of expectations when we know we can meet new expectations without exception at that new level.

Further, we pledge to:
- Know who our customers are and what they expect.
- Have visibility into every corner of the organization so that people always know how their job affects customer success, and when that success is threatened.
- Immediately respond when customer success is threatened.
- Aggressively pursue the elimination of events that can unintentionally reset customer expectations or create new ones.
- Communicate our experiences in delivering success to help identify opportunities for improvement and risk elimination.

While this mission statement is generic in the sense that it does not tell us what the business does, it is specific in telling us what the people in the business do. This generic mission statement clearly communicates what is expected from the people in the organization at every level and in every role from a strategic perspective. There is no ambiguity and no opportunity for conflicting priorities. We are in the business of setting and meeting customer expectations—with "we" being everyone in the organization. The premise behind this customer oriented business approach is a set of Truths—ten to be exact.

The 10 Essential Truths of Customer-focused Companies:
1. The business *is* Customer Expectation Management: setting customer expectations and then meeting those expectations without exception.
2. For the business to be successful, customer outcomes must be successful.
3. We must understand what expectations our customers have, what success means to them.

4. We must know who our customers are *before* we can define these expectations.
5. The customer is not always right, but the customer can always be successful.
6. Our success is achieved in the delivery of customer success without exception.
7. Success is delivered by people—not by technology, policies or management.
8. Everyone in the organization must have the information necessary to act for customer success.
9. Everyone in the organization must have the authority to act for customer success.
10. Everyone in the organization must be held accountable for customer success.

The translation of these business truths to actionable statements results in the Customer Success Mandate that sets the foundational criteria for delivering customer success.

The Customer Success Mandate:
- Directly support the delivery of customer outcomes that meet customer expectations.
- Include the concept of successful customer outcomes as a real-time, actionable and measurable entity.
- Include the ability to express the success entity as a set of success elements that are measurable and actionable.
- Include the ability to determine real-time failure of the process outcome whenever the process fails to meet a success element.
- Incorporate the concept of meeting customer expectations without exception.

- Deliver the information necessary to act for customer success to everyone in the organization involved in the associated outcome.
- Resolve decision-conflicts so that people can act for customer success.
- Include the real-time flexibility for decision-making to be adaptive on the scene.
- Include the ability to identify success threats and inform process participants and managers.
- Hold everyone in the organization accountable for customer success.

But how do we express "success" as determined by customer expectations? How do we act on it? What is meant by failure of the process to produce success—and how do success elements fit into the picture? How can we be expected to inform, resolve decision-conflicts, have real-time decision flexibility, identify threats, and hold everyone in the organization accountable?

The answers to these questions form the basis for building the hyper-competitive business.

The Hyper-Competitive Business

Transforming the business into a hyper-competitive business sounds daunting and the questions uncovered in the discussion of Mission Statements would seem to represent a very significant challenge that imposes a substantial (costly and painful) requirement for organizational change. Nothing could be further from the truth.

There is work involved, that much is true. And change is required, but the change burden rests on a select minority of professionals in the business. The requirements for meeting customer expectations without exception are three-fold.

Meeting Customer Expectations Without Exception:
1. We must orient ourselves to the inclusion of customer expectations in our strategic plans.
2. We must build out strategy by identifying the detailed set of interaction points, their metrics and the criteria that determines success.
3. We must provide the organization with the means to act on this for success.

Returning to the layers of the customer-focused enterprise diagram, we see that it visually shows three "layers" in the customer-focused enterprise. The top layer is focused on strategic vision and creativity. The middle layer takes the strategic customer outcome, identifies the fine-grained elements that make-up success and focuses on aligning the organization from top to bottom in direct operational relationship with strategy. The bottom layer is focused on operation and management including refinement and optimization.

One of the big *traditional* challenges faced by any organization is the coordination of efforts by all of the people in the organization in alignment with strategy. Hierarchies of every type create versions of goals or localized goals at all levels that may (or may not) actually support the overall strategy of the organization.

The meeting of customer expectations *does not suffer* from

this effect because the business approach to customer expectation management makes an inherent connection between strategy and the activities of people.

Layers of the Customer Focused Enterprise

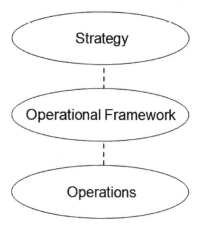

The ability of a business to become a hyper-competitive business rests on the success definitions for customer interaction points. These definitions (regardless of how they are actually expressed) must include the expectations, associated metric(s), and criteria for determining success or failure.

Yes, the definitions do task the organization with identifying all of the customer expectations for each interaction. Yes, to succeed does require the identification of metrics for each expectation. And yes, the criteria for determining the success or failure for each expectation must also be identified.

How else can we make successful judgments, take appropriate actions, and empower employees to achieve success?

This set of information is *the* information that enables the people in the organization to directly relate to strategy, take action in alignment with strategy and self-measure their own success or failure in the performance of their job. How much simpler can change be?

Of course it is not *that* simple, but this does convey another very important benefit of approaching customer success in this way. Any time people have clearly defined goals, are given a measurable target they can understand, the criteria by which it is judged, and resulting judgments (even if they make the judgments themselves) they have a clear means to act. Education and training, typically a significant time and resource burden, is negligible because the links to corporate strategy are not implied, they are explicit. Goals have no ambiguity. Actions are clearly defined. Measures are known and success criteria are documented. Every person in the organization who interacts with a customer is in alignment with corporate strategy. They know what is expected of them, what constitutes success and what actions must be taken to achieve success. There is no confusion, no conflicting priorities and no "translated goals" that reflect a restructured functional view of what someone in the organizational hierarchy *thinks* corporate strategy really means in their domain.

The links to corporate strategy are not implied—they are explicit.

The power of the hyper-competitive business rests in Customer Expectation Management and that means meeting customer expectations without exception. This is far different from the traditional management approach that is focused on the goods or services offered by the business. The hyper-competitive business is a successful business because of its ability to execute on the new CEM elements of the 21st century value chain (not on margin). Explicitly linking strategy to the actions of people with expectations, metrics and success criteria is the backbone of the hyper-competitive business, enabling the business to extract the maximum revenue and profitability possible from the current value proposition of the good or service. This implies that the hyper-competitive business can execute on almost any given product or service with success—and that is exactly the case.

Cellular Service – Virgin Mobile USA. We reviewed the redefining of the value proposition for cellular service with Virgin Mobile USA earlier; now let's look at the Virgin Mobile USA value chain.

Virgin Mobile entered the USA market in 2002 without installing, owning or maintaining a single cellular tower or the infrastructure required to deliver cellular service.

As of February 2005 Virgin Mobile USA laid claim to 3 million customers—and it still does not own or operate a single piece of cellular service infrastructure.

There are two parts to the Virgin Mobile USA story.

From Virgin Mobile USA: "Virgin Mobile also continues to provide outstanding service that exceeds the expectations of its customer base. Over 90% of Virgin Mobile customers say they'd recommend the service to a friend-while more than eight-in-ten (83%) already have recommended Virgin Mobile to a friend or family member (Source: MSI Survey of current customers, 4Q 2004)."

"In addition to high marks for customer referrals, Virgin

Mobile also keeps its gold-star status for customer satisfaction. Recent independent research among current customers gave Virgin Mobile a 92% satisfaction rate. 'Customer service is our most important measure of success,' Schulman said."

Virgin has accomplished this with more products than just cellular service. From magazines to mail order records; record stores, recording studios and a record label; to film and video distribution...; to airlines, trains, e-commerce and mobile phones—Virgin has applied the concepts of the 21st century value chain to its business with a degree of success that most business people can only stare at in envy.

Yet the realities of the 21st century value chain can be leveraged by any business, even if it doesn't have a "Sir Richard Branson" at its helm.

Let's look at an example of a fictitious business we will call Budget Airline to explore the implications of this further:

The Budget Airline Example. Budget Airline offers "no-frill" low-cost airline travel. Its business model focuses on meeting or beating the competition on price, coupled with simplicity of the "experience." The value proposition is low-price, no-hassle air transportation.

Starting at the strategic level of the business, Budget Airline must define the customer expectations it fulfills with its value proposition. Then, it must identify the associated metrics—the criteria for determining success or failure based on those customer expectations.

There are two parts to the Budget Airlines value proposition: *low price* and *no hassles*. For low price, the strategic expectation is that Budget Airline's pricing for the travel destinations it covers will be the lowest prices available in the industry.

The metrics associated with the "low price" expectation are the prices of competitors for the destinations served by Budget Airline. Using information updated multiple times daily from ATPCO (Airline Tariff Publishing Company), Budget Airlines has the metrics against which it can deliver on this customer expectation.

However, remembering that the goal is meeting expectations without exception, Budget Airlines recognizes a gap exists in real-time competitor pricing information between each update from ATPCO. The customer expectation (as set by Budget Airline) is that Budget Airline will provide the lowest cost for the destinations it covers.

As a result, Budget Airline institutes an automated pricing system that uses the rates from ATPCO, a secondary (ongoing) research function that audits pricing during the gap periods and a pricing scheme that prices its flights at its target margin rate or one percent below its lowest competitor—whichever is *lowest*. Budget Airlines uses this pricing scheme to achieve two goals, the first being the delivery of lowest price without exception, and the second being the delivery of pricing that is significantly lower than its competitors to help attract new customers and keep existing customers. This helps achieve competitive differentiation.

Though Budget Airline recognizes the need to review this approach regularly to detect any changes in competitor behavior that could threaten its delivery of the lowest price expectation, the practice currently yields consistent results at greater than 99.9% success against expectation.

When Budget Airline began working through the *no hassles* part of its value proposition it immediately recognized it had a decision to make. Should Budget Airlines internally define what *no hassles* meant—limiting that definition to the elements it felt was important *and* that it knew it could deliver on? Or should Budget Airlines comb through its business to determine what the real master set of sub-expectations (all customer interactions) was for inclusion in a model that truly delivered no hassle service? Budget Airline chose the latter.

The examples below show how expectations for delivering on a *no hassle* experience developed and were implemented.

Check-in: To have a *no hassle* experience at check-in, Budget Airline identified customer expectations as being both *simple* and *quick*. The company found that one metric applied to *quick* (time) while multiple metrics applied to *simple*.

Reviewing the expectation of *quick,* Budget Airline determined that 15 minutes was considered a *normal* wait time for customers desiring to check-in with a ticket agent's help. To address this expectation, Budget Airline identified where the 12 minute point was in the line and placed a specific sign there that its employees could easily recognize. Budget Airline then identified the wait in line as a Moment of Truth, identified MOTs as the priority work for *all* employees, added a red MOT button at all ticket stations, and linked the MOT button to the break room, pagers and radios of its employees.

The Moment of Truth Threat occurred anytime the line reached the sign (the 12 minute mark). Ticket agents were identified as the "Threat Sensors," with the missive to press the button anytime the line reached the 12 minute point—and for other ticket agents to respond to the threat as a priority. The button does not get reset until the line drops below the 12 minute point, providing a success or failure measure that the company tracks and reports to employees. Achieving success at this Moment of Truth only required clear prioritization for employees and the low-tech means to sense and respond to threats.

Now, before looking at some other examples of what Budget Airline did it is important to know that Budget Airline issued this new action information under a new set of documents entitled "Corporate Strategy—Success without Exception." At the time these documents were distributed, Budget Airline also informed employees that performance (success or failure) of MOTs had been added to all employee reviews—as the top priority for assessing employee performance.

Another expectation Budget Airline identified was how long customers had to wait to claim checked baggage. Budget Airline found that customer expectations varied widely, typified by a general expectation of *too long*. Considering the time required for de-boarding the plane and to walk to the baggage claim area, Budget Airlines was able to determine that a time of 25 minutes from plane dock would be an expectation that—if met without exception—would qualify as success for its customers.

The approach to addressing the baggage delivery requirement differed substantially from the approach to address check-in. With baggage claim, it was quickly obvious that the issue was one of understanding and prioritization. The baggage handling group was given the Corporate Strategy—Success without Exception document outlining their Moments of Truth. The time for plane dock was already being recorded in Budget Airline's information systems, so it now added the measure of when baggage unloading was complete. The baggage group (they were tasked with finding their own solution) added large LED signs with flight number and a countdown of 22 minutes automatically triggered by plane dock. This easily enabled baggage staff to know exactly where they stood against their Moments of Truth. The final action taken by the baggage staff was a set of large signs that proclaimed "It's not success until it's in the passenger's hands" to keep the group alert to any problems with the baggage delivery system itself. The outcome from this simple step yielded over 98% success against goal (mechanical failures being the primary cause for failure).

On an entirely different front, Budget Airlines recognized that "no hassles" meant proactive communication to its customers—a point that came from the recognition that mobile alert use was on the rise but still represented only a fraction of Budget Airline's customers. As a proactive means to help customers avoid any hassles, Budget Airlines added two new services. The first service allowed customers to receive automated phone call alerts for delays and gate changes while the second service allowed customers to give Budget Airlines their phone number so that the company could use caller ID to give custom information *anytime* a customer called. Customers who signed up for this service and called Budget Airlines were immediately told pending flight information for themselves or flights they had marked as needing monitoring, including gate information, current flight status, and any delays or changes *without* having to listen to any automated menus or make any menu selections.

These are examples of how the fictitious Budget Airline might have gone through its organization to determine Moments of Truth with its customers, how the company identified metrics and what criteria for success were used in determining success or failure with customer expectations.

Now this example is not intended to be an accurate representation of what a real budget airline would identify for success and only presents a small sample of the real elements of success that would be identified, documented and then acted on. But it does illustrate the point that success in a customer interaction has multiple points where expectations, metrics and criteria for success can be identified. This is something very few organizations have looked at in detail but the expectations of customers are found in the details of customer interactions, and it is the expectations of customers that are the measuring sticks for customer success or failure.

Much of the challenge in aligning people with process comes from the difficulty in relating work activities back to the strategic goal of the process (and business). Instead, people commonly work within systems that dictate their actions by business rules, system configuration or administrative mandate that just don't make the connection back to strategic goals. The result is that people perform their work within a micro-bubble, and just don't worry about customer success. This condition is exacerbated by limited visibility into the effects from their actions on the "bigger picture." They are disconnected, disenfranchised "workers" who have no reason or foundation helping them to achieve customer success.

That's not to say that people in the business do not work, because they certainly do. People perform their jobs as best they understand them but they have no "skin in the game." They have no ownership, feel little responsibility and expect no authority. The all too familiar result is a workforce characterized by "robotic" behavior that falls into repetitive patterns,

patterns that all too frequently fail to support strategic goals.

In comparison, the hyper-competitive business becomes a customer-focused enterprise inherently engaging people in the strategic goals of the business. If we wish to drive actionable strategy throughout the organization that immediately begins producing customer success then we must produce a framework that enables and empowers people to act for success. This is the success without exception framework.

Success without Exception Framework:
- Identify each expectation
- Identify the metrics of the expectation
- Determine the criteria by which success or failure is determined
- Track metrics, successes and failures
- Communicate expectations, metrics and success criteria to affected employees
- Provide success metrics to affected employees (in real-time where possible)
- Provide employees with the means to *succeed*
- Track and communicate success threats wherever possible
- Where possible, provide employees with the proactive means to respond to success threats prior to the success or failure result
- Use success results as the primary means of assessing (and rewarding) employee performance

Let's return to the discussion of Budget Airline for a moment. In the Budget Airline example, we reviewed several of the steps taken by Budget Airline to help the company deliver success on their value proposition —*low cost* and *no hassle*. The *no hassle* portion of the value proposition was chosen to help present a very important point about the nature of the hyper-competitive business. As it turns out, if we take the term *no hassle* at its meaning without adding any "fine print" it closely mimics customer success defined as "every expectation at every point of customer interaction," except perhaps with a more aggressive set of expectations than what customers already expect from airlines (redefined customer expectations).

The Budget Airline example illustrates the power of the hyper-competitive business.

Budget Airlines – A Hyper-Competitive Business. In the fictitious Budget Airline example, we now jump to the stage where Budget Airline has propagated the meeting of customer expectations without exception across all customer interaction points.

This includes every customer point of entry (internet, phone, in person, self-service machines) evaluated to determine each element of each interaction that has a point of success or failure, the metrics and criteria for each, and the means to track and present results to the people in the organization. This includes incorporation of these elements into the corporate strategy (Corporate Strategy—Success without Exception), methods to detect success threats and the means to respond to those threats before they lead to failure. Employee performance evaluation is tightly bound with success as defined by corporate strategy.

Budget Airline now delivers a high level of success without exception for most customer interactions. The only real exceptions are those where the customer either a) cannot success-fully communicate to Budget Airline what they are trying to accomplish or b) the customer expectation is simply something Budget Airline can not (or will not) deliver (which means the expectation is outside the value proposition).

If we think about how this impacts us, the customer, we uncover the fact that Budget Airline has made our lives much easier and simpler. It is easy to interact with Budget Airline because we experience success and it is simple because the experience is repeatable. We know what is going to happen at each interaction point and the consistency of results allows us to focus our attention on other matters. The number of variables in our lives has just been reduced, eliminating a source of stress. Activities we engage in before and after our flight have become simpler and more manageable by the reduction in variables and variation as well.

The Budget Airline value proposition comes from two elements, low cost and no hassles. In this example, Budget Airline successfully delivers on its value proposition, addressing the requirements of the 21st century value chain. However, taking a closer look at Budget Airline reveals another important aspect.

The first part of the Budget Airline value proposition, low price, is delivered by the success process of checking competitors' pricing. Using available industry pricing information, additional price information Budget Airline gathers, and analysis to make its decisions, Budget Airline has developed the ability to accurately determine what constitutes "lowest price" for all of its flights. Budget Airline's ability to offer low pricing is driven predominately by operations in the margin portion of the value chain. The business rule is that margin activities must enable

Budget Airline to operate flights at the "lowest price" and still make a profit.

Meeting customer expectations without exception in pricing is a simple process, automated with an audit function that requires little effort. The effort to deliver on this part of the value proposition while remaining profitable comes from the margin portion of the value chain just as Porter originally defined it. So in the case of low price there has been very little new work, process or control added to the activities of the organization beyond traditional value chain management.

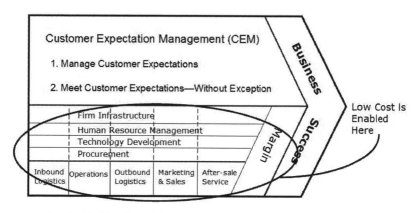

The 21ˢᵗ Century Value Chain

When we look at *no hassles*, the picture is much different. Now we see that value chain effects exist *exclusively* above the level of the margin portion of the value chain.

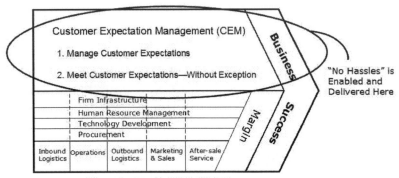

The 21st Century Value Chain

In the case of Budget Airline, the company has identified expectations, metrics and success criteria that enable the explicit support of strategy by people in the organization. Inclusion of metrics tracking and reporting gives employees real-time insight into their *personal* success just as aggregated metrics give management (at all levels) insight into success at the group, division and organizational level.

The result is an organization that works in far greater harmony towards a common goal. Inclusion of success/failure results (directly from strategic goals) in employee performance evaluations reinforces business goals, sets clear work prioritization and fuels motivation. The approach shunts off the typical political and hierarchical complexities faced by classical management approaches and builds unity of purpose that feeds on itself because the organization has a clear call to action. Opposing forces (sub-goals, translation through hierarchy, personal agendas, non-synergistic functional goals) are either blunted or effectively removed from having any real effect on the actions and priorities of the people in the organization. The work people do is now explicitly linked to the strategic vision of the business.

Because Budget Airline committed to the proper use of this approach it became a hyper-competitive business. Further, the commitment to meeting customer expectations without exception produces a degree of resonance in the business through real-time feedback in direct alignment with strategy. This "feedback loop" motivates people to success, and success motivates greater success (and so on).

So what happens to a business that applies this approach to become a hyper-competitive business? In the case of Budget Airline a deep change has occurred within the business that opens the door to new opportunities for business growth.

By meeting customer expectations without exception, Budget Airline has created a real competitive edge in its business. Looking back to the original value proposition—low cost, no hassles—we must recognize that low cost is not a defensible business position. Low cost is a margin game, one where the variables and intricacies of the delivery of airline service are well-established and deeply analyzed. What one airline can do on margin another can do as well. The only real low cost competitive advantage exists in relationship to larger, established airlines that must undergo longer change cycles to reform operations to the low cost model against their existing legacy environment. Yet even this holds only a temporary competitive advantage. If the need is there, even established competitors can transform margin activities quickly (for example, American Airlines has responded to real budget airlines with pricing that now typically beats even the most aggressive of these margin competitors).

The Margin Game—Learning from the Airline Industry.
The advent of low cost, or budget airlines, has filled a niche in
the market that over time has propagated out in the market to
cause widespread change throughout the industry. Airlines such
as Southwest, AirTran, and Jet Blue have triggered price contraction industry-wide as their volume and success have grown, spur-
ring their larger full service cousins to react with competitive pricing to retain market share. That response, though arguably too
little and too late for *some* of the larger carriers, has arrived and
the outlook for the smaller low cost airlines is no longer as bright
as it seemed to be as little as a year ago (2005).

Has the low cost airline opportunity already popped? This
may well be the case. With revenues and profit showing substantial flattening, the growth (and business success) of the low
cost smaller airlines now seems to be in jeopardy and is certainly under competitive pressure.

Consider American Airlines, the nation's largest airline car-
rier. Feeling the pressure of discount airlines and recognizing
the impacts from loss of customers, this US airline giant has
adopted an aggressive program of price competition that has
kept its planes full and retained its customer base while striking
into its margin chain to reduce operating cost with a venge-
ance. Customers flying American Airlines will now find pricing
more than competitive. In the majority of cases, if a route is
served by American, then American will offer one of the best
prices for your flight—including the prices of the "discount"
or low cost airlines.

In an industry where size, volume, infrastructure, employees
and cost complexities are staggering, if the largest of the

"older" model airlines can reinvent itself to compete with the "new" model airlines designed and streamlined for low cost competitors it should be obvious that competing on margin alone is *not* a long term competitive opportunity.

The New Budget Airline. In the discussion of Budget Airline, we have observed the setting and delivery of the value proposition including low cost and no hassles. However, "no hassles" taken forward as the widespread execution of success without exception yields more than just a competitive edge on the customer front. Budget Airlines has produced an organization that can deliver success without exception—a real competitive advantage—that bears no relationship to "low cost." The low cost part of the value proposition of Budget Airline is for budget air travel. The ability to deliver success without exception applies to any business, market or target Budget Airline wishes to pursue.

This gives Budget Airline the opportunity to target other market demographics and customer profiles. If Budget Airline decides to spin out a brand called "Comfort Airlines" that deals with a less price sensitive market that expects an expanded customer experience its hyper-competitive business is already geared to deliver on the value proposition by simply identifying new expectations and incorporating them into strategy guidance with expectations, metrics and measures. The work to accomplish this mainly lies in the defining or redefining of the value proposition and the identification of actionable expectations, metrics and success criteria (along with any additional equipment and/or services needed for the new value proposition). The implementation of the new value proposition has now become the easy part of the equation, as the people in the organization are already well-prepared to act on new strategy. Presented as expectations with metrics and success criteria, new strategy falls seamlessly into the activities of the organization as nothing more than a modification or extension to what they are already doing.

Virgin is a company that has tapped into much of the power of this approach, though the company has developed this capability the hard way. From humble beginnings as a mail-order music business, Virgin has developed a customer-focused enterprise over the years that meets expectations better than most companies and has leveraged this strength to expand into numerous markets—most of which are not even remotely related to the music business.

Virgin moved from mail-order music to the creation of the Virgin music label, distribution of film and video media, games—and then air travel (commercial and public), hotels, distribution, trains, radio, cellular phones, and more. The success of many of these business ventures is tied to the fulfilling of customer expectations. Virgin is noted for making "customer to business" interactions easy, simple and even fun.

Virgin is an example of the organic development of a customer-focused business, an approach that requires superb leadership, management and employee training. While Virgin has done (and continues to do) it right, the challenge faced by the Virgin approach is too great for most companies.

Within the fictional case of Budget Airline, we see the creation of customer-focused capability that rivals Virgin, accomplished with a highly pragmatic approach that does not require superb leadership and management. By leveraging the new element of Customer Expectation Management in the value chain, any business can become a hyper-competitive business. Success without exception (once expectations, metrics and success criteria are identified) provides the framework for creation of hyper-competitive capability in any organization under a controlled (and controllable) approach. This is the opportunity for business success and the approach to achieving hyper-competitiveness becomes even clearer when we look into the idea of hyper-competitive processes.

Hyper-Competitive Processes

Customer success is at the heart of business success in the 21st century but the power of success without exception is more than just the identification of expectations, metrics and success criteria.

Remember, customers are not kings; they are dictators. Every failure to meet a customer expectation creates the motivation for the customer to seek out our competitors.

In light of this fact, it is important to realize that customer interactions are dependent events. Every customer interaction is part of a larger set of interactions, a set of interactions that is best viewed as a process.

This aligns with the practices arising from the application of business process management (and its derivations). Business process management focuses on identifying the work performed in the organization as a set of processes that have a beginning and an end where that end has a specific outcome.

Each customer interaction follows a process. Very few interactions have only one expectation, instead being a composite set of interactions (and expectations) required to achieve a specific outcome.

David Berlind (executive editor of ZDNet) has experienced this, and written about his experiences under the mantra of "Customer Moments of Truth," (a term attributed to Jan Carlzon while at Scandinavian Airlines in the 80s resulting in the book of the same name).

In one article, "Are you blowing your 'customer moments of truth?," David notes several key realities of customer interactions in regards to an experience he had with Nextel. David notes the statement of Steve Mills (IBM Senior Vice President) from an earlier interview, "Every customer contact is a moment of truth for a business."

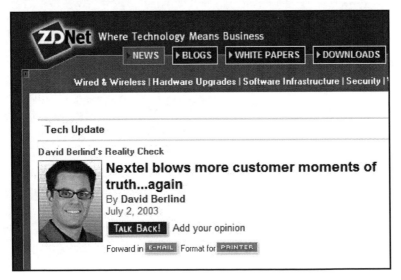

David then goes on to comment, "How many times have you been the victim of a customer moment of truth gone awry?

Dozens? Hundreds? Thousands? How many times have you walked away shaking your head at just how badly some store or company screwed up when you were the customer? Better yet, how many stories have you heard from friends, family, or colleagues about failed customer moments of truth? Now add up the dollars, the loyalty, and the customers lost. Those poor, stupid businesses--some of them long gone and not a moment to soon. Is your company the next poor, stupid business?"

This is followed by the recounting of an experience with Nextel showcasing how Nextel failed him on multiple expectations in a single customer interaction.

This highlights the fact that customer interactions typically include multiple expectations, each being a success or a failure—a Customer Moment of Truth. For customer success to be achieved, success is required at each of these Moments of Truth.

This is a radical change from how we traditionally think about and manage the operations of the business. Functional separation of the business and hierarchical management structures zero in on portions of the customer interaction, not the entire customer interaction process.

When properly developed, the business process management practices of defining and redefining value propositions include the identification of Moments of Truth, but typically stop short of incorporating these Moments of Truth into actionable directives that become part of the daily management of these processes.

Even with the process-centric approach of business process management technology there is currently no embedded capability to address the control or management of customer interactions at Moments of Truth because the process models used in BPMS products are not designed to address this aspect of the business. They can (even within existing products, though as a "one-off" design technique), but they don't because BPMS products remain focused on process flow and the process model for customer success is *not* a flow model.

The Customer Interaction Model. The model behind customer success is not flow-based. Instead, customer interactions are evaluated as the composite of all interactions that occur with the customer during the process that yields an outcome for the customer. Stealing from the Boolean algebraic system of logic based on work by mathematician George Boole in the 1800s (that became the foundation of electronic circuit design and later for computer processing) the customer interaction model is effectively a Boolean logic "and gate."

The "and gate" has one (and only one) output but it can have an unlimited number of inputs. It performs the logical comparison that if (and only if) *all* inputs are true (successful) then the output is true (successful). There is only one way to make an "and gate" give a "true" output and that is for all inputs to the gate to be true at the same time.

The "and gate" in customer success is the domain of any one interaction between the customer and the business. The domain of a customer interaction is the scope necessary to meet what the customer perceives as an interaction. This domain will usually include multiple expectations (again, from the customer's point of view). The customer success model "and gate" shows us that if (and only if) all inputs (individual expectations) are successful will the customer interaction itself be successful.

This means that any *failure* on an input in the customer success model will produce a resulting *failure* of the interaction—i.e. customer success will *not* be achieved.

Why is success measured against such unforgiving criteria? Think about interactions that you have had where you are the customer. What do you remember? Do you remember the four things the business did right? Or do you remember the one thing they did wrong? What do you talk about to other people? The business that did what you think you should reasonably expect them to do? Or the business that failed to do what you expected?

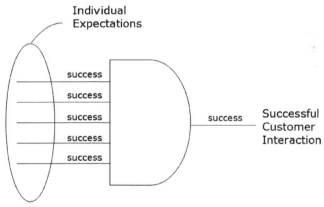

Customer Interaction Model – AND Gate

Back to the underlying truth of customers, anytime we fail on any part of an expectation that failure is what sticks with the customer. It is human nature that we remember those things perceived as negative—and to retain them far longer than those things perceived as positive. Neutral perceptions are ignored. Interaction success is not getting three out of five expectations right, or seven out of ten. It is not about nine out of ten. It is about ten out of ten. Anything less than 100% will encourage customers to consider other choices and to seek ways to abandon their relationship with us.

For many, the idea of applying such unforgiving criteria to the operation of the business may seem daunting. It would seem that the goal is beyond the ability of what we can achieve. Yet on further review, the "and gate" provides the definitive model to achieve success without exception. There is no ambiguity, there are no conflicting purposes and there is complete visibility into results. Because the hyper-competitive business has explicit goals, defined with metrics and success or fail criteria, we know what we need to do and we have direct feedback on our success towards those goals.

Remember, the goal is business success. Indirect, relative or indicative success measures provide a basis for management activities, but they don't show us what is really happening in the organization, nor do they provide the means to achieve real success. Application of the "and gate" process model can uncover failure to meet expectations that individually may seem low, but actually create a high customer expectation failure rate.

Customer interaction success is achieved by knowing what must be done to achieve success on each expectation, having the means for accurately (and directly) measuring it, and taking action to achieve success on every customer expectation. When expectations are documented and backed by metrics and success criteria, they are actionable and measurable. Approaching customer success from traditional management practices produces nice numbers that hide the underlying failure rate as shown in the following diagram.

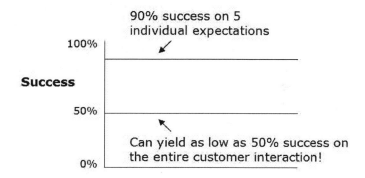

AND GATE EFFECTS

Identifying all of the expectations for a given customer interaction with the "and gate" process model enables organizations to:

- Gain a clear view of success (or failure) for each customer interaction
- Bridge the "gap" between functional areas by providing a common measure of success (the entire interaction)
- Operate against *real* measures for determining success or failure for customer interactions
- Push accountability onto the effective success or failure of the interaction process (the "and gate") as opposed to just individual expectations
- Measure and reward performance outside of functional areas (again, the entire interaction as represented by the "and gate")
- Drive work, priorities, and actions from direct success metrics in real-time (not assumptive or historical analysis)

Hyper-competitive processes can take things even further. Using the "process paradigm," businesses can develop a "sub-process" definition for each expectation. Perhaps the use of the term sub-process is not entirely accurate, but the point is that for each expectation the characteristics of a process are represented and can be employed to manage the activity behind the expectation. These characteristics include the statement of the expectation, the metric(s) used to assess results of the expectation and the criteria that determines success or failure. Depending on the specifics of the expectation, available technology, and capability for event detection; these activities can include threat detection, failure avoidance, escalation, and remediation.

When we consider the flow-based process model used in BPMS products we see a classical definition that each process has a starting point, n number of steps and an end point where an outcome has been produced. This facilitates control and management of the process outcome and the activities performed at individual steps of the process. But it does not include the measurement and analysis of individual activities at steps where those activities include interaction with the customer—where such interaction (in and of itself) has an outcome that should meet the customer's expectation at that point in the flow.

This can be a difficult concept for those versed in process modeling using technology. It is rarely the case that these interaction points (each of which is a Moment of Truth) are currently viewed as having the characteristic of success or failure. Further, it is even less common to include this practice on all customer interaction points. Including customer interaction points as Moments of Truth with success or failure judgment and determining customer success as the composite of all MOTs in an interaction is the "missing link" in current BPM practice and technology.

But hyper-competitive businesses must include this perspective if they are to achieve business success. This "perspective" is an additional model for directly engaging the people in the organization in the delivery of success without exception.

Having suggested earlier that each customer interaction within an overall customer expectation can be likened to a "sub-process" in the customer interaction model, that concept bears further scrutiny. What other elements can (and should) exist in the sub-process definition for a customer interaction?

Threat Detection and Failure Avoidance. Threat detection is the ability of systems or people to identify when there is a threat to success on a given expectation. Threats occur when results from metrics indicate an abnormal condition—typically the failure of some detectable condition that is normally met in interactions with customers when producing success. A threat is a probable indicator that success will not be achieved, occurring before the judging of success or failure. Failure avoidance is the response to threats that moves these interactions back into the likelihood of success.

Threat detection and failure avoidance can be as simple as documented guidance helping people in the organization to recognize threats and to guide them in a successful response— all the way to advanced use of technology that includes detection of multiple threats, threat levels, programmed alerts and process or rule based programmatic response to avoid failure.

Escalation is another technique applicable to some interactions, escalating interactions under threat to higher levels for assistance in achieving success. Interactions that have a longer time-period are more likely to benefit from escalation. Because hyper-competitive processes are grounded in the strategic directives of the business, escalated interactions already have passed the "noise bar" (it is common for people to use escalation when they are uncertain, wish to avoid responsibility, are having a bad day, etc) because they are being escalated as part of the process directly supporting business strategy. Escalation may still exist for a number of reasons, but escalated interactions are driven entirely by corporate strategy or mandate. There is no ambiguity for these escalations. They are bona fide threats to the success of the business.

Even remediation can enter into the picture. There will be times when failure occurs, it cannot always be avoided. Remediation can be included in hyper-competitive processes to produce a response when a failure occurs that communicates to the customer several important things, including:

- We know we failed you
- It is important to us that we failed you, and we want you to know *that*
- You are important, and it is worth our time and effort to know when we fail to meet your expectations
- We take this seriously, and expect our business to deliver success to you
- We wish to highlight the importance of our relationship with you by providing you with a token of our appreciation as a sign of our commitment to success without exception

Remediation can take many forms. As a rule, it is unnecessary to provide a token of appreciation (though it may be warranted or may be used to reinforce sincerity). What customers really want when a failure occurs is to know that the failure was noticed, that it (and they) matter to the business, and to have confidence that the failure is the abnormal (not normal) result they can expect. Timely acknowledgement of failure communicates in no uncertain terms that the business recognizes it has failed the customer, that this is not an acceptable situation from the business's point of view (we already know it is not acceptable from the customer's point of view) and reaffirms the fact that the business has a real commitment to success for the customer. It is an earnest apology that rings true for hyper-competitive businesses that are constantly improving on the level of customer success they deliver.

Hyper-competitive processes can include remediation, again ranging from the recognition by people that a remediation action is appropriate to use within systems that determine various remediation steps or actions based on any number of real-time and historical (typically customer history) information, events, logic and rules. The permutations are important, for when statistical anomalies occur (we average one failure per customer per year but John Doe experienced nine this year) it is in the business's best interest to take exceptional remediation action.

This means that within a hyper-competitive process there may be multiple events raised, that events can trigger a variety of actions, probable failure can be detected with actions that deliver success before the failure occurs (including escalation of the interaction to appropriate levels), and where a failure does get through the process—trigger a remedial action that can be based on context (including customer history) to acknowledge the failure in a proactive manner.

Process definitions for interactions including expectations, metrics, success or failure criteria, event sensing, threat recognition, threat response, real-time visibility, and remediation in hyper-competitive processes all combine to produce success without exception. The degree in which businesses adopt these techniques within their organization determines the magnitude of sustainable business success realized by the business.

Let's look at a couple of basic process examples to clarify this further. Taking a look at the traditional flow-based process model graphically provides clarity on the start point, *n* steps and end point structure of flow-based processes.

Traditional Flow-based Process Model

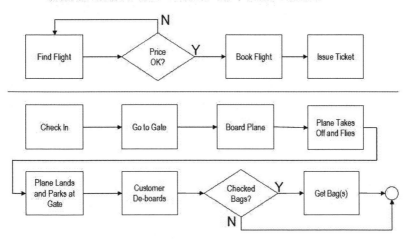

In the process model presented in the diagram above, activities are presented as an ordered set of steps having a clearly defined start and end. Included in this diagram is one example (checked bags) of flow control where alternative process routing can occur depending on the state of current conditions. The traditional flow-based process model diagram presented here shows two distinct processes.

Taking the steps of the flow-based model perspective with applied Moments of Truth and the success without exception customer interaction model provides an entirely different view of the same process.

MOT to Flow Modeling Relationship

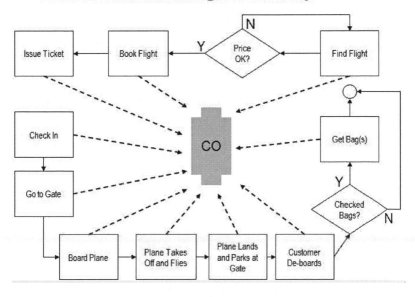

In the diagram above, the dotted lines represent those steps of the original flow-based process where a Moment of Truth exists. For each step of the original two processes, all steps with associated Moments of Truth have been included in relationship to the customer outcome (CO).

But wait a minute! Why are two processes suddenly represented by the same customer outcome?

The reason for this is a problem common to flow-based processes, the tendency to look at the process from the "inside-out" rather than the "outside-in" (the customer point of view). It turns out that these two processes are fundamentally perceived as one process in the perception of success or failure by the customer.

This diagram also clearly depicts the fact that flow is not how customers perceive—and judge—their interaction with the business. Each step where customer interaction takes place is a success or failure point in the overall interaction with the customer and failure at any one of these points produces failure to the customer.

Drilling into more detail on how these Moments of Truth are managed (and why they can be a sub-process) can be shown by the example of what happens when the process includes proactive response to an impending customer failure.

Moment of Truth Threats – Proactive Response

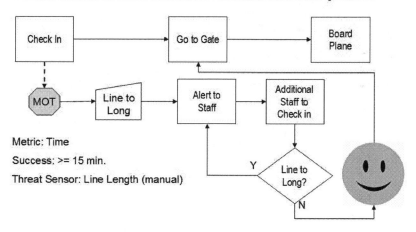

In the proactive response model presented above, we now see that a sub-process really can exist for a given Moment of Truth. In this case the Moment of Truth is the length of time customers wait at the check in step of the airline process. The sub-process shows how expectations, metrics and success or fail criteria can be used to create actionable sub-processes that trigger response to impending customer failure before that failure occurs.

In the case where failure simply cannot be avoided there is another form of sub-process that can come into play in the customer interaction model. The remediation process for the check in step of the airline process might look like this:

MOT Failure Remediation

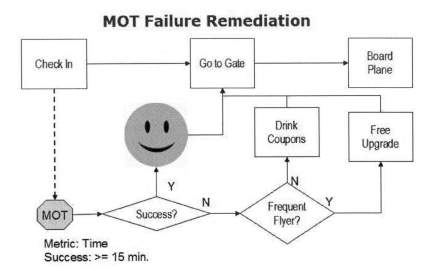

Metric: Time
Success: >= 15 min.

Regardless of how they are implemented, it is this type of model that allows the people in the organization to directly engage in providing customer success on every interaction between the business and the customer.

Hyper-Competitive Processes and Partners

An important aspect of many hyper-competitive processes is their need to include or encapsulate business partners. In every customer relationship there should be only one business that owns that relationship. Companies that choose to allow joint ownership of the relationship in either active or passive mode give away their customer mandate, subjecting the business to undue (and unwarranted) risk that can threaten the very existence of the business. This risk falls clearly outside the boundary of reasonable corporate governance yet the taking of this risk is in evidence in corporations of all sizes and markets at a staggering level.

For example, consider the practice of mail-in rebates. Manufacturer mail-in rebates are used to increase volume of transactions at the point of sale on one hand while most of these programs are operated on a rebate avoidance basis on the other. From the customer point of view, this practice is purposefully and intentionally fraudulent. In this scenario, there can be no customer success. Mail-in rebates often cast the customer relationship into jeopardy for a business that within its own organization does a good job of success without exception. Though some businesses may rightly note that it is the manufacturer (in most of these cases) engaged in avoidance tactics (not the retailer or seller), that doesn't matter to the customer. In the customer's eyes, the mail-in rebate problem is directly associated with the retailer they do business with. The built-in customer failure of rebate practices lands squarely on the retailer's shoulders, not the manufacturer.

When partners exercise this type of behavior—behavior that obviously falls infinitely short of the goal of success without exception—the onus is predominately placed on the seller, not the partner. Customers buy a product with a rebate (even if the rebate is a manufacturer's rebate) and when the fine print, side stepping, and other avoidance procedures kick in to defraud the customer of their legitimately earned rebate the customer is more likely to begrudge the seller—not the manufacturing partner. Is this the way to achieve success without exception and drive the growth of the customer lifecycle? It is certainly not.

Some companies have begun to understand the impacts of

the new value chain and the effect on customers from partner behavior.

Best Buy. Best Buy, a leading electronics and appliance retailer has committed to the elimination of all mail-in rebates by April 2007—while staunchly defending the opportunity for customers to get bargains by replacing mail-in rebates with instant rebates. Best Buy is serious about this aspect of success without exception, having already eliminated 65% of the mail-in rebates by April 2006 (as compared to those that had been in place the year previously). Best Buy *understands* that failure by manufacturers to make their rebate process simple, fast and easy results in its customers' inability to achieve success. Because Best Buy understands the importance of customer success, it has taken aggressive steps with manufacturers, forcing them to be "partners in customer success."

A byproduct of this particular action in support of success without exception is the perception of Best Buy's customers beyond the delivery of success. Many Best Buy customers see this action by Best Buy as advocacy for success on their behalf. It is interesting to note that when success is not achieved, the "blame" routinely falls to the first business in line (like retailers) but when success like the rebate scenario is addressed by the retailer, not only is customer success achieved but the retailer is accorded special merit for taking up the cause of the customer. For Best Buy the win is on two fronts (success and advocacy).

When partners are involved in the goods or services a business offers to their customers, these partners, their activities, their performance, and their success must be tightly woven into the hyper-competitive process model. In the pursuit of success without exception, partners must play on the same playing field as the business with the same clarity of strategy (and commitment), the same visibility in success or failure, and the same stringent analysis (and compensation) of their performance against the meeting of customer expectations without exception.

Hyper-Competitive Metrics

When hyper-competitive processes are employed, the ability to manage the organization to success without exception is enabled through hyper-competitive metrics. This is another attribute of the explicit linkage to strategy in the hyper-competitive business. Hyper-competitive metrics provide direct, real-time indication of the success (or failure) of the organization against the goal of success without exception.

Hyper-competitive metrics provide the visibility at every level of the organization to know exactly what the current and historical state of success and failure is within the business.

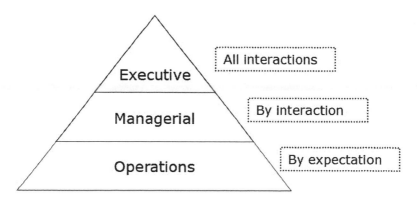

Hyper-Competitive Metrics

Based on the "and gate" model for hyper-competitive processes, these metrics provide:

- The overall success and failure rate for all customer interactions with the business
- The success and failure rate for each customer interaction
- The success and failure rate for each customer expectation
- The success and failure rate for each customer

The "chain" of causality for hyper-competitive metrics provides a simple, yet powerful, analytical capability for identifying just where failure stems from, or better, where opportunity for improvement lies. In looking at the basic attributes of hyper-competitive metrics it can be seen that even those with little or no training in business analysis can quickly identify problem areas and isolate the source of the failure.

Consider the retail furniture industry. In general, the industry has suffered for some time now from low profitability, high customer turnover and financial woes for even some of the biggest retailers in the industry.

How do they manage their business? Of course it varies, but far too often furniture retailers operate with distinct functional boundaries. Many of these retailers focus on marketing, competitive pricing, sales, and sales gimmicks. There is often a distinct transition that occurs from the "end" of the sales process to the actual receipt of goods that closes the transaction. It is clear that the metrics used to manage these companies rests on traditional sales and margin analysis with little (if any) connection to customer expectations.

Reviewing a common furniture retailer model in both the

traditional form of operation and then as a hyper-competitive business using metrics for the analysis provides the contrast necessary to understand the importance of hyper-competitive processes and hyper-competitive metrics.

The traditional model approaches the customer interaction process as one of sales and fulfillment, with sales being the strategic activity used to manage the organization.

Traditional business analysis would look at sales from numerous perspectives, breaking down with a resulting activity report that might look something like this:

Sales Report by Store	
Total number of sales	362
Total sales value	$261,726
Average sale price	$723
Average gross sales $ per salesperson	$29,081

This high level sales report would then be broken down by date, time, salesperson, store, region, territory and so on. The report is focused on the business, more particularly on the sales area of the business where performance incentives are directly linked to individual salesperson's sales results. There is nothing about the customer here other than the number of customers and the sales they yielded to the business.

But what is really happening in the business? Are customer expectations really being met? Is the business really capitalizing on its customer pipeline? Are they maximizing the customer lifecycle? The traditional form of business operation does not provide the metrics required to answer these questions.

From the hyper-competitive process perspective, the new customer process is indeed a process, one that has numerous customer expectations associated with it. Looking at this same set of organizational activities from the hyper-competitive process perspective would yield information in a much different form and relationship.

Customer Success	
Price	89%
Selection	74%
Sales process	69%
Purchase process	54%
Delivery process	39%
Pick up Process	44%

Looking at this report provides sudden insight into the effects on actions of the organization that are not part of the traditional management approach. The retail furniture industry is fraught with process issues that often start the moment a customer decides to make a purchase. Though the percentages presented here are for illustration purposes only, the fact remains that the business and customer relationship hinges on those activities that occur after the sale (fulfillment) rather than before or during the sales process itself.

How many people will refer us to their friends and neighbors in the scenario presented above? The reality is—not very many.

How many people will look forward to extending their relationship with us through the purchase of additional products?

Well, we have given most customers reason to *not* do business with us again so how can we expect them to return? Instead, we have referred our customers to our competitors so extending the relationship with the customer now hinges on the judgment that we are the "lesser of two evils." Is these how we build customer relationships?

Will our customers actively consider alternatives to us? Of course! We have failed to make them successful, to keep their lives simple and easy, and by so doing we have motivated them to look for a business relationship that does serve these needs.

Hyper-competitive metrics can easily be broken down by other attributes such as day, time, department and employee to better analyze what is happening in each process. Further, each of the "processes" depicted above can be broken down to their individual metrics with success or fail criteria capable of explicitly directing the activities of everyone in the achievement of customer success.

With hyper-competitive business, the information (and understanding) of how customers are being affected changes dramatically to include a number of new insights into the operation of the business including:

- Why potential customers are being lost at numerous expectation points in the process
- How the customer views the relationship as compared to how we (the business) view the relationship
- Where the best opportunities lie for us to improve on our delivery of customer success
- What the real scope of failure is from the customer point of view

Comparing the two business metric scenarios just pre-sented, it becomes clear that in the first scenario there is no visibility into the disconnection between company measures and customer measures. In the second scenario, with customer interactions, expectations, metrics and success or fail criteria developed and tracked, visibility into real business success is available at all levels of operation and management.

This new information uncovers the real impact of opera-tions on business success. In the traditional operating scenario, accurate information was available but that information did not convey the results of operations on the primary factors that affect business success. Decision-makers in traditional margin-based operating businesses do not have the information needed to identify those areas where improvement can yield business success.

The quality of decisions is based on the accuracy, complete-ness and appropriateness of the information used to make those decisions. The use of hyper-competitive metrics places the right information, in the right relationship, in real-time, into the hands of front-line employees all the way up to organiza-tion-wide strategic management—directly enabling the highest quality decisions at every level of the organization.

The Danger of Unrepeatable Positive Outcomes

We have discussed in detail the importance of meeting cus-tomer expectations without exception, how to determine suc-cess or failure, and how the delivery of success without excep-tion is a driving force behind business success in the twenty-first century.

Yet there is another issue with customers that is even more overlooked than the success or failure of expectations. This issue may appear to be benign but in reality can exert negative pressure on the customer relationship. This issue is the delivery of unrepeatable positive outcomes (positive anomalies).

Positive anomalies are those situations where everything goes *right*, producing an unrepeatable, but positive, outcome at a Moment of Truth. This is a good thing, or is it?

In traditional business thinking, the focus is often on achieving a degree of success or result from activities and processes. Management practice and technology are geared towards avoidance of failure. Even when the data required for analysis of exceeding goals is available it is rarely brought out as information unless it directly relates to organizational or individual performance goals.

Returning to Budget Airline, let's consider a case where a positive anomaly could occur:

- Check in – If the Moment of Truth metric measure of success is 60 minutes (instead of 15) travelers will plan accordingly for their arrival time at the airport. If we suddenly deliver an outcome at the check in Moment of Truth of 5 minutes, how does this affect the customer?

- The customer is now at the airport with 55 minutes of "extra time" to fill prior to boarding. This will certainly get their attention and will likely be considered an *inconvenience*.

- We have also stated to the customer that we *can* complete their check in experience in 5 minutes, not 60 minutes. Even when there is a logical explanation as to why the time needs to be 60 minutes—and this is truly an anomaly—the customer perception is often... "if you can do it in 5 minutes this time then you should be able to do it in 5 minutes *every time*." What we have done is *reset* the customer's definition of *success* to a level we cannot provide on a repeatable basis.

- Plane Arrival – If the Moment of Truth is to arrive at the destination airport in no less than 10 minutes longer than the scheduled arrival but we arrive at the airport 15 minutes ahead of schedule how does this affect the customer?

- First, what if we cannot move (workflow) to the next step in our process, docking at the gate? To the customer, we have landed and are ahead of schedule. This is likely to produce a slightly positive feeling with the customer. However, if the customer must now wait on a gate to be ready, sitting out the *earlier arrival time* in the plane *on the ground,* we immediately produce a *negative* feeling. This is a *failure* because we have created a new expectation (success is defined by expectation) by arriving early, and then produced a *failure* against that expectation because we really haven't arrived at the gate earlier.

- Second, in the case where we are able to dock at the gate immediately we have now arrived at the airport earlier and that could disrupt plans to meet someone (they aren't there yet) or meet an unidentified need of the customer because they are on a tight schedule and we have helped them (inadvertently)—and thereby created another unplanned expectation: I will arrive early.

These examples give simple illustration to the basic concept behind the potential negative effect that positive anomalies can cause. These examples bring out certain characteristics that are rarely considered when defining and implementing business processes. In many cases, the best business processes:

- Recognize the success of the customer outcome is at risk in most steps of a process.
- Identify Moments of Truth and empower their organization at all steps of their processes through prioritization of work against MOTs where MOTs exist.
- Offer a repeatable customer experience that eliminates events that can cause the customer to *reconsider* the service being provided—both positive and negative events.
- Recognize the unwarranted and unnecessary risks associated with creating new customer expectations, and align activities to avoid creating new expectations, and the resulting redefinition of the successful customer outcomes for the process.

Positive anomalies produce an unrealistic expectation with the customer. The worst case scenario of this is the "escalating expectations syndrome" where businesses deliver an unrealistic positive outcome that the business does not desire to deliver as part of their value proposition to the customer. When this happens, the unrealistic outcome can become the new customer expectation. When this emerges as a pattern the resulting expectation of the customer is "I expect you to exceed my expectation," a syndrome that will force failure as a breakdown when the business eventually collapses under the stress of this impossible cycle of increasing expectations without end.

But even simple positive anomalies are a danger to the business. Any time success is met outside the bounds of what the customer expects—and the business commits to deliver—this causes the customer to reconsider the relationship, or at least to reconsider their expectations from the relationship. Yet we have shown that the best customer relationship diligently avoids those conditions that cause the customer to think about the relationship. The longest lived customer lifecycles come from relationships where the customer is given no reason to consider or reconsider their relationship with the business.

The human mind only focuses on those things that are different from what was expected. Intelligence theory (such as presented in Jeff Hawkins' "On Intelligence"[7]) shows that the human mind has different levels of "processing" where cognitive awareness occurs in greater degree at higher levels of "processing" only when associations fall outside of expected patterns. At the lowest level, where associations very closely match the expected pattern, the brain works on virtual autopilot. Business relationships that operate on this level are never subject to scrutiny nor do they rise to a cognitive level—they just are. The brain is happy that the associations match the expected pattern and as long as the match does not have an associated negative connotation the result is that we simply have no active awareness of the event at all.

Positive anomalies force our minds out of this level of auto-acceptance because the patterns don't match and this pushes the event up to one of the cognitive levels of thinking. Suddenly we are aware of the event, we think about it and our brain's natural process adds this unrealistic positive outcome to its association with the pattern.

Cognitive awareness and association of outcomes to patterns is true for both positive anomalies and failures.

Prosumer Processes – The New Frontier

A trend in business practice that will heavily impact the 21st century value chain is the emergence of the prosumer. A prosumer is a customer that engages with the company in self-service mode, the interaction being conducted by the customer and the company's systems.

The prosumer model has come into vogue as a byproduct of Internet capability and availability. We all know that we can now shop online for anything and many businesses allow us to retain accounts with them that have details about us, our preferences, and stored information to reduce the time to complete transactions.

Prosumption is a step beyond this initial use of the Internet for the customer to business relationship. Consumers will interact with the business in self-service mode, not to simply make buying choices or to set preferences, but to engage with all of the product or service offerings of businesses. These prosumers will build the very nature of the customer/business relationship as a unique expression of their personal goals and desires. The prosumer model exposes the business as a map with many destinations, routes, choices, and combinations that represent the superset of all customer/business relationship combinations possible.

In this model, customers will find the unique relationship that best serves their needs. The model presents two requirements that businesses must deliver against, an interactive prosumer model that enables customers to follow their unique motivations in their own way to easily find and build a customer relationship profile that best meets their needs exactly how they perceive those needs, and the ability for the customer to do this with success without exception .

Call it Web 2.0, Business 2.0, whatever you like. The reality is that the breadth of the customer-business relationship is restricted more by the customer's lack of awareness of products and services that meet their needs (and combinations that meet their needs in ways that truly help them achieve their goals). A constant limitation imposed on the customer-business relationship rests in the lack of understanding or awareness of products and services the customer needs that they do not know are available from the business.

There are many factors involved in this problem, with the greatest challenge resting in how a business enables prosumers to express their desires in a simple, natural way that builds on itself over time. The challenge is further complicated by the need for success without exception. Customers that are frustrated early on by a prosumer interface that does not enable them to achieve their goals will quickly drop the relationship down to the basic level until they can switch to a different business for the goods and services desired.

The ClueTrain Manifesto.[8] A book that took the world by storm (with the book of the same name released in 2000 that ranked number 6 on Business Week's list of business bestsellers and number 9 on Amazon's list) presents a vision of what the Internet is really triggering across the globe – an entirely new channel of human conversation:

"In many ways, the Internet more resembles an ancient bazaar than it fits the business models companies try to impose upon it. Millions have flocked to the Net in an incredibly short time, not because it was user-friendly – it wasn't – but because it seemed to offer some intangible quality long missing in action from modern life. In sharp contrast to the alienation wrought by homogenized broadcast media, sterilized mass 'culture,' and the enforced anonymity of bureaucratic organizations, the Internet connected people to each other and provided a space in which the human voice would be rapidly rediscovered."

This "conversation" is a new form of interactive human experience that includes within it new forms of interaction with businesses in the awareness, selection, purchase and consumption of goods in the broadest sense.

Though corporations insist on seeing it as one, the new marketplace is not necessarily a market at all. To its inhabitants, it is primarily a place in which all participants are audience to each other.

Meeting customer expectations without exception takes on a new dimension in this regard. In the prosumer model, this portion of the value chain now includes the ability of the business to enable prosumers to find services, products and services, plus product combinations that:

- the consumer does not know the business has,
- they do not know that they want,
- they do not know even exist,
- or that they are not looking for from the business.

Financial institutions are a great example here. The products and services available from financial institutions are broad, customizable, and often interrelated. Banks that start customer-business relationships with checking accounts are seldom able to communicate to their customers the variety of services they have to offer. Simple interfaces that allow customers to make simple choices that tailor the interaction to the customer's goals, present pertinent products or services and that help customers choose the right products or services to achieve their individual goals is what prosumers must be given. Maximizing the customer relationship rests on success without exception where meeting customer expectations without exception is now augmented by enabling the customer to find those products or services combinations that best help them achieve their personal goals.

Though it may seem daunting, this emerging prosumer model represents a boon to businesses that get it right. The investment required for successfully implementing the success without exception prosumer experience applies to all prosumers, those that exist already and the ones to come. The prosumer experience offers the opportunity for expansion of the customer relationship under a model that outsources the work to the consumer. A powerful concept, indeed!

Amazon.com. Amazon.com is an example of a company engaging in the prosumer model. Though much of what Amazon has now does not incorporate customer success as it should, the overall interactive capabilities of the online "Amazon Experience" are a step in the right direction.

At Amazon, the customer experience is personalized with a mixture of user settings that characterize the interests of each user and prompt digital conversations through the sharing of consumer lists, preferences, and reviews. The experience is further enhanced with the automated presentation of related products and services that align with each consumer's choice, including those selected by Amazon and from other Amazon consumers (people who bought this book also purchased…).

Amazon has further expanded the ability to create many different interactive person-to-person experiences with their release of a comprehensive set of web services that enable partners to prepare their own "flavors" of interaction for customers and "smart" accounts that tailor the Amazon site to the individual that is using it.

Certainly the models for achieving real prosumer capability are complex and in their infancy. Yet the application of success without exception to prosumer models forces the prosumer model onto the straight and narrow path to success for customer (which produces success for the business). Application of expectations, metrics and success or fail criteria to prosumer interaction models pushes the organization towards the needs of the customer while providing the feedback needed to know what portions of the prosumer model are successful and which have failed.

Becoming a Hyper-Competitive Business

So how does one become a hyper-competitive business? . What steps must be taken, and where do I start? Here are a few to get things started.

Identify your Customer Outcomes: Becoming a hyper-competitive business requires that customer outcomes be clearly understood. What customer outcomes does your business deliver? What elements make them competitive? What elements are essential, and which ones are not? How does what you deliver equal customer success?

Understand the Process Behind Outcomes: Once we know what customer outcomes we deliver, and the elements that make up the delivery of those outcomes, the next step is to characterize the process behind the outcome. Do we know the process behind the outcome? Is it clearly understood as a holistic process, rather than a functional set of activities?

Know the Customer's Expectations: Outcomes and the processes behind them are then reviewed from a different perspective, the customer perspective (outward-in). What does the customer expect? What constitutes success in the eyes of the customer? How have we made the customer's life simpler and easier? What are we failing to do that would make the customer's life simpler and easier that is a reasonable expectation in the eyes of the customer?

Uncover all Customer Interactions: We must also dig deeper into the activity of the business to identify all those places where the customer interacts with the business. What interactions could happen for a given outcome that we have not already identified? Have we captured them all? Do we understand what they are and why they exist? Have we scrutinized them to see what is necessary and what exists due to poor design on our part or to address failure at other activities in the business?

Make Success Actionable: Identify expectations with metrics. Measure them. Identify success or failure criteria. Measure this too. Communicate this to the organization. Empower them to deliver success. Give people clearly actionable goals that can be measured and judged with the freedom to create their own success. Do this and they will succeed.

Reward Success: Tying performance evaluation and compensation into the picture at an early stage is critical. This, *more than anything else*, provides the motivation to the people in the organization to act on the delivery of success as a priority in their daily work. Saying "success without exception" is important has little meaning. Placing success without exception at the heart of employee compensation undeniably states the importance of this to the business and its leaders.

Do, Learn, Grow, Expand: The hyper-competitive business is one that is continually moving closer and closer to 100% success. Much like quality initiatives, the goal is continual improvement on the success percentage, pushing it closer and closer to perfection. This includes expectations and interactions. Over time, the hyper-competitive business refines itself in the delivery of success without exception while expanding its *success domain* to all customer expectations and interactions. No matter what degree of success is achieved, there is always room to grow. Make sure you are growing.

Become Proactive, not Reactive: Learn to recognize change and change agents that will cause a shift in customer expectations. Work to become a market leader, not a market follower. Be open to new customer expectations and new variations of old expectations. See these changes as opportunities, not as threats or burdens. Know that the customer outcomes your business delivers must be fluid, not rigid, so that you can respond in the right way at the right time to deliver customer success on an ongoing basis.

Building a hyper-competitive business is not rocket science. It requires commitment, attention to detail, and a strong desire to deliver customer success. Don't make exceptions, look away

134 Customer Expectation Management

from difficult issues, or delegate responsibility to someone who does not understand the importance or believe in the value of the practice. Solid adherence to the principles behind the hyper-competitive business will deliver business success.

Remember that the starting point for building a hyper-competitive business is the customer expectation. The customer expectation begins with the touch point where a customer first "touches" the organization.

How might customers touch the organization? If the business has "brick and mortar" stores, then it may be the moment the customer enters one of these stores. It could be a phone call, an email or a visit to a website.

Businesses should look at all of the ways in which a customer can touch the organization. Can customers walk into your store? Can they call you on the phone? Do you have a website they can interact with you at? Do customers contact you via email, instant messaging, direct mail, or through sales people?

Always remember that the outcome for an expectation is the customer outcome from the customer's point of view. The outcome for each expectation must be described from the outside-in.

This entire activity is focused on the point of view of the customer, not on the needs of the business or on an idealistic concept of what the customer process should be. The goal is to document what the customer expects so that we can build the means to deliver on that expectation. In most cases the organization is already performing most (if not all) of the activities required to meet the customer expectation. The activities are just not reliable or consistent enough to meet the customer's expectation on a repeatable basis. They are not reliable and consistent because we have not been able to communicate to the people in the business how their activities create success, or failure. We have not empowered them to achieve success.

Of course, we must make sure we know what the customer expects from us! It is all too easy to slip away from the outside-in view, to put things back into the content of the business. If we take the customer process model, metrics and the criteria for determining success we can build a composite customer success statement that represents what we believe the customer expects from us:

"I came to your store, found the high definition television I wanted in less than 20 minutes, you had it in stock, you brought it out in less than 10 minutes, it took less than 5 minutes to purchase it, there were no hidden charges, there were no "mail in" rebates, you had someone help me load it into my car (and I didn't have to wait)."

The importance of capturing customer success in this way provides the means to review what we believe is the customer's expectations as if they were telling that expectation to us:

- Does this reflect the point of view of the customer?
- Does it sound right?
- Is there anything obviously missing?
- Is there closure (did we capture the end-to-end process)?

Many Ways to Achieve Success. But how do we drill down into the often complex workings of an organization to identify, document, innovate and implement success without exception?

The first place to look is at internal practices that have already been developed and used with success in addressing other organizational challenges.

Does your organization have a business process management program? What about Six Sigma, Lean, Kaizan or TQM? Improving the ability of the organization to deliver on success without exception can come from any of these types of practices. These disciplines have the inherent capability to address specific success requirements at the group, team, department and even the functional levels.

If your organization doesn't have any of these types of practices, consider project management. Does your organization have skilled project managers? In smaller organizations, who is the "go to person" that gets special projects done? They may be the person who needs to lead this activity.

The point is that improvement becomes an activity common within most organizations. The rule is simply: *use the talent and capability within your organization that has already proven its ability to achieve your goals.*

A Controlled Approach: It should be no surprise that only a controlled approach will yield success. Incremental adoption is often the best practice, where the organization builds its success on experience. Some organizations will target only a few expectations that are well understood initially.

As success is achieved and experience is gained, the ability of the organization to roll out the practice throughout the organization will grow. Success leads to the ability to create success, and success without exception in one area will lead to success without exception in another.

However, it is important to remember that even when we

deliver success on every interaction but one, more customers will remember that one failure than all of the successes combined. Hyper-competitive businesses deliver success on all customer interactions. Getting there in stages is fine, but going part way then stopping is a recipe for business failure, not business success.

Get Started. These guidelines can help any business get started on the road to becoming a hyper-competitive business. The approach you take may vary from that presented here in any number of ways, given the context of your business and market pressures. As long as the approach drives the business toward success without exception (and keeps going that way) the benefits are there to be had. Exactly *how* you get there is far less important than *getting there*.

References

[1] Successful Customer Outcomes (SCOs) are further described in articles by Steve Towers at www.stevetowers.com.

[2] From the book *Extreme Competition*, by Peter Fingar

[3] source: IDC (International Data Corporation)

[4] The American Banker's Association

[5] Sprint PCS (company press release 4/15/02)

[6] Los Angeles Times (07/25/2001)

[7] The book *On Intelligence* by Jeff Hawkins (Time Books)

[8] The ClueTrain Manifesto (www.cluetrain.com), *The ClueTrain Manifesto* (book), Perseus Books Group, authors by Christopher Locke, Rick Levine, Doc Searls, David Weinberger

Index

2

21st century value chain, 20
21st Century Value Chain
    Realities, 56

A

Airline Tariff Publishing
    Company, 85
AirTran, 96
Amazon.com, 130
American Airlines, 96
and gate, 102
and gate process model, 105
average customer acquisition
    cost (ACAC), 53

B

Berlind, David, 100
Best Buy, 116
Boolean logic, 102
Branson, Richard, 84
Business 2.0, 128

C

Carlzon, Jan, 100
cellular phone number
    portability, 27

CEM, 19, 20, 21, 29, 40, 48,
    49, 65, 66, 68, 83
Chevrolet, 23
Cingular, 24
ClueTrain Manifesto, 128
Communications services, 48
Customer Expectation
    Management, 14, 19, 20,
    21, 28, 29, 65, 71, 77, 82,
    98
Customer Interaction Model,
    102, 103
Customer Lifecycle Extension
    (revenue), 62
customer pool, 43
customer relationship, 35
customer service paradigm, 19
Customer Success Mandate,
    78

D

Dell, 68
DHL, 71
Discount Tire and Auto, 44
Drucker, Peter, 14

E

Economic demand, 14
enemy is failure, 36

escalating expectations
   syndrome, 125
escalation, 107

F

Failure avoidance, 107
Federal Express, 69
four factors of customer
   focused success, 39

H

Hotmail, 48

I

IBM, 100
Increased Loss to Profit
   Transitions (revenue), 59
industrial revolution, 14
instant rebates, 116

J

Jet Blue, 96

L

law of supply and demand, 13
Layers of the Customer
   Focused Enterprise, 30
links to corporate strategy, 82
low cost, 92
loyalty chain, 23

M

mail-in rebates, 115
Management by Expectation, 14
Management by Objectives, 14
Margin Game, 96
Mills, Steve, 100
mission statement, 76
Moment of Truth, 86
Moment of Truth Threat, 86
Montgomery Wards, 22
More New Customers
   (revenue), 57

N

New Customer Value Chain
   Effects, 56
Nextel, 100
no hassles, 93

O

On Intelligence, 126

P

pay as you go service, 73
Porter, Michael, 17
Positive anomalies, 123
process trigger, 134
prosumer, 127

R

Redefining of Customer
    Expectations, 65
remediation, 108
Repeatable Delivery of
    Customer Expectations, 80
retail furniture industry, 120

S

sales gimmicks, 118
Scandinavian Airlines, 100
Sears, 22
Service contracts, 27
Skype, 49
Southwest, 96
Sprint PCS, 24
Star Wars, 16
Success without Exception
    Framework, 90
sunspots, 24

T

Ten Commandments of the
    Customer-Focused
    Enterprise, 12
Ten Essential Truths of

Customer Focused
    Companies, 77
Threat detection, 107

U

UPS, 71
USPS, 71

V

Verizon, 24
Virgin Mobile, 72
Virgin Mobile USA value
    chain, 83
volume and price market
    dynamics, 17
Vonage, 49

W

Walmart, 68
Web 2.0, 128
World Wars I and II, 14

Z

ZDNet, 100
Zero Sum game, 19

About the Author

Terry Schurter is Chief Analyst of the BPM Group, the world's largest not-for-profit business process management community (www.bpmg.org) and is co-developer of the 8 Omega Framework for business process. He is a noted authority on BPM technology, and a thought leader in the practice of business change, strategy and emerging business challenges.

Terry has consulted with numerous businesses on strategic management, directed numerous integration programs for fortune 500 companies and is the recipient of two George Westinghouse Signature of Excellence awards for process engineering innovation with nuclear material management systems.

He is a contributing author for *In Search of BPM Excellence* and *Technologies for Government Transformation* (Government Finance Officers Association, 2005) and is a popular speaker at both business and technology conferences and events around the world.

Terry lives in the Dallas, Texas area with his wife, Christy, and their two miniature schnauzers Rufus and Cricket.